SOUTH SHORE BOOKS 164 PITT WEST
WINDSOR, ON N9A 5L4 (519) 253-91[illegible]

1 0198692307 G 25.50 = 21.68 [illegible]

DISCOUNTED 15.0%
QUESTIONS OF ENGLISH

SUB-TOTAL	21.68
GST	1.51
TOTAL	23.19
CASH	25.00
CHANGE	1.81

[illegible]
[illegible]

YOU'RE KIND OF SORTED OUT IN LIFE
IF YOU READ ENOUGH GOOD BOOKS.
- HUGH GRANT -

Questions of English

Questions and Answers about English Words,
their Origin, Use, and Meaning,
from the files of the
Oxford Word and Language Service

Questions of English

Compiled and edited by

Jeremy Marshall and Fred McDonald

Oxford New York
OXFORD UNIVERSITY PRESS
1994

Oxford University Press, Walton Street, Oxford OX2 6DP
Oxford New York
Athens Auckland Bangkok Bombay
Calcutta Cape Town Dar es Salaam Delhi
Florence Hong Kong Istanbul Karachi
Kuala Lumpur Madras Madrid Melbourne
Mexico City Nairobi Paris Singapore
Taipei Tokyo Toronto

and associated companies in
Berlin Ibadan

Oxford is a trade mark of Oxford University Press

Published in the United States
by Oxford University Press Inc., New York

British Library Cataloguing in Publication Data
Data available

Library of Congress Cataloging in Publication Data
Data available
ISBN 0–19–869230–7

1 3 5 7 9 10 8 6 4 2

Typeset by Hope Services (Abingdon) Ltd.
Printed in Great Britain on acid-free paper by
Biddles Ltd., Guildford and Kings Lynn

Contents

Acknowledgements

The material for this book is in large part based on the correspondence files of the Oxford Word and Language Service, and we are indebted to every member of the English Dictionary Department who has been involved in the OWLS at one time or another during the last ten years. We are especially grateful for the recent efforts of Juliet Field, Simon Hunt, Sarah Hutchinson, Rosamund Ions, David Shirt, Edmund Weiner, and Tania Young, and for the support of John Simpson and the indefatigable Margot Charlton.

1

Introduction to the OWLS

The Oxford Word and Language Service (OWLS for short) was launched by the Oxford University Press on the Ides of March, 1983. The Dictionary Department had always received numerous enquiries from dictionary users, and it was felt that the service should be regularized. The first enquiries began to arrive almost before the ink was dry on the press release, and since then the lexicographers have answered a truly enormous number of queries about the origin, meaning, and use of English words.

The questions come from university lecturers, schoolchildren, word-game enthusiasts, foreign students, secretaries, translators, monks, historians, pensioners, lawyers, and many others of extraordinary variety. Some are puzzled by a word or expression that they have come across in reading, or heard on the radio, or remember their grandparents using. Others have been entangled in arguments with friends or colleagues about the use of words. Queries arrive on anything from picture postcards to impressively crested notepaper, and from backs of envelopes to faxes. They are answered using the computerized version of the complete *Oxford English Dictionary*, the research files and electronic databases of the Dictionary Department, and the collection of dictionaries and other reference books kept in the Department library.

Most of the letters we receive are a great pleasure to read and answer. Many people have a deep enjoyment of words and of the English language, and it is a delight to share it. Few things are as satisfying as finally tracking down the solution to some intractable problem of word origins, or identifying some obscure word found in an old will, or discovered in an ancient recipe book, or remembered from the conversation of an elderly relative. Nevertheless, we sometimes have to admit regretfully that we do not know the answer to a query.

Not all our correspondents seem to have appreciated the limits of our expertise, though we were able to give some help to the enquirers who wanted to know where to buy rhinestones, and how to play hunt the slipper, and we have sometimes been able to trace quotations. More than once we have been asked, in very polite but extremely convoluted English, if we would please send the writer a free copy of our dictionary in return for eternal gratitude.

> God bless you and guid you please I bend down when I'm writting this letter to you. Please I need your aid, something like gift. 'Cos I like your company.

Other letter-writers have more general information to convey:

> Yesterday I recieved a present for my birthday. The present is a Pocket Oxford Dictionary. I really like it alot thank-you very much for inventing them. I got other things for my birthday. Please can you write me a letter back sending souveniers (thats if you have any). Thank-you very much.

Some people write to us in the (vain) hope that we will help them to win a competition, or do their school projects for them, or read their novels, or answer their English homework. Others send huge lists of questions, or long series of postcards, or ask more and more difficult questions about obscure points of literary interpretation or linguistic philosophy. We have had to explain that we are an English Dictionary department, and cannot necessarily claim any great expertise in Welsh, Japanese, or Sanskrit, though we can sometimes pass on queries to scholars in various fields. Our work is concerned with English words, and we can usually offer little help with foreign terms not used in English, and only limited help with proper names.

It must also be said that many of the questions we receive could easily be answered in fifteen minutes in the reference section of a public library, from works such as the *Encyclopaedia Britannica*, *Whitaker's Almanack*, the *Guinness Book of Records*, Debrett's *Correct Form*, or indeed from the *Oxford English Dictionary*.

We are often obliged to explain that dictionary definitions do not themselves have any legal authority (though they are often cited in court cases), and that we do not provide legal advice. We can advise on the meanings of words in ordinary use, but legal definitions are determined by the courts.

To many of our correspondents 'the Oxford Dictionary' is the ever-popular *Concise Oxford Dictionary* (**COD**), first produced in 1911 by H. W. Fowler (later to become famous as the author of *Modern English Usage*) and his brother, F. G. Fowler. To us, however, the phrase means the complete *Oxford English Dictionary* (**OED**), which in its second edition runs to twenty large volumes. Originally conceived as a dictionary to contain every word in the language, it was begun by the Philological Society in the middle of the 19th century. The first sections appeared in 1884 under the editorship of James (later Sir James) Murray, who soon had to give up his teaching post in London to devote himself to the great dictionary in a 'scriptorium' he had built in his garden in North Oxford. This was gradually filled with slips of paper bearing dated quotations from all kinds of English text, sent by numerous industrious readers, and sorted by Murray's assistants and members of his family. (Over five million slips were amassed. Most of the original ones still exist, but they are extremely fragile and are kept by the Bodleian Library in Oxford. Some were sent to other dictionary projects such as the *Middle English Dictionary* after completion of the *OED*.) The story of Murray's work on the dictionary is told by his granddaughter K. M. Elisabeth Murray in her book *Caught in the Web of Words* (1977).

By the time the dictionary was completed in 1928 it had three more chief editors (Henry Bradley, Sir William Craigie, and Charles Talbot Onions) and ran to ten volumes (twelve in the reprint of 1933), yet the language was developing at such a speed that complete coverage was clearly never going to be attainable. A supplementary volume was published in 1933, and then four volumes of the *Supplement to the Oxford English Dictionary* were produced between 1972 and 1986 under the direction of Dr Robert Burchfield. The entries from these supplements, together with additional newly researched material, were combined with the earlier text to produce the 20-volume second edition, published in 1989 and now also available in electronic form on CD-ROM. Plans for a third edition are now taking shape, and an appeal to scholars for material was published in 1993. Meanwhile a series of *OED Additions* volumes is beginning to appear.

An abridged version of the first *OED*, sharing its historical emphasis but lacking the huge mass of cited evidence, was published in 1933 as the *Shorter Oxford English Dictionary*, and this became well loved as a scholarly dictionary affordable by the individual reader. In 1993 the *New Shorter Oxford English Dictionary* (**NSOED**), an entirely revised edition incorporating the results of research not available to earlier editors, was published in two volumes. It aims to include all the words in general use in English from 1700 to the present day, tracing their history back as far as it is known, as well as covering the vocabulary of Shakespeare, Milton, and the King James Bible.

The Oxford University Press now also produces a wide range of other dictionaries, from the weighty *Oxford English Reference Dictionary* through the *Pocket* and *Little* dictionaries to the diminutive *Oxford Minidictionary*. Each includes as much information as can be crammed into the available space. Other dictionaries are designed for the needs of a variety of users, from the *Oxford ABC Picture Dictionary* to the *Oxford Dictionary for Scientific Writers and Editors*. There is the *Oxford Large Print Dictionary* for those with poor sight, and dictionaries of specialized vocabulary in a wide range of subjects, from computing to sailing, medicine to music. There are dictionaries for foreign students learning English, from *Start with Words and Pictures* to the *Oxford Advanced Learner's Dictionary* (used all over the world), and a number of bilingual dictionaries.

Many of these dictionaries now bear on the inside of the cover the figure of an owl, and an invitation to write with queries to the OWLS at Oxford University Press. And that is where we came in . . .

2

What is the origin of . . .?

Q What is the origin of the ENGLISH LANGUAGE?

English, like most European languages, is a member of the Indo-European family. The Indo-Europeans are believed to have lived in Eastern Europe or Western Asia, probably somewhere around the Black Sea, some 5,000 or so years before Christ. Gradually they spread eastwards into the Caucasus and northern India and westwards into Europe. Through this common ancestry English is linked to languages as diverse as Sanskrit, Latin, Gaelic, and the Scandinavian tongues. English belongs to the Western Germanic branch of the family; its closest relatives are German, Dutch, Frisian, Yiddish, and Afrikaans.

For convenience we use the terms **Old, Middle,** and **Modern English** for the forms of the language spoken at different times. While these terms refer to significant linguistic periods, they do not mark sudden changes but stages of gradual development.

Old English was the language spoken by the Anglo-Saxons. There were several major dialects; most of the literature that survives is in the Wessex dialect. Like modern German it was a moderately inflected language, using endings added to the word stem to indicate the part the word played in the sentence, its grammatical gender, and whether it was singular or plural. It is on the whole incomprehensible to modern readers. Old English was influenced by the Scandinavian language of the Vikings; this was Old Norse, in many ways similar to Old English but with its own grammatical system and inflexions. As Danish and Norwegian settlers became naturalized Old English started to lose its inflexions. Then the Norman invasion began the temporary ascendancy of French, and by 1150 Old English was effectively obsolete. The last entry in the Anglo-Saxon Chronicle was made in Peterborough in 1154.

Middle English, which emerged in the twelfth century, was strongly influenced by French and Latin and had begun to lose its inflexions. The early forms of it are extremely difficult for the modern reader, but the later forms, the language of Langland and Chaucer, can be understood with some effort and a glossary for words which have not survived. (The reader will also need some imagination and flexibility of mind, as spelling was extremely variable.) Dialects were still important and distinct.

Middle English developed into **Modern English** somewhere between 1450 and 1500 (1470 is sometimes used as a conventional cut-off point). The invention of printing did much to establish this new and more standardized form of English, which passes without a distinctive break into the language we speak today. The Midland dialect, spoken in an area which included London, Oxford, and Cambridge, formed the basis for what we now call Standard English. Sixteenth-century English—the language of Shakespeare and the Book of Common Prayer—is not radically different from our own. **Thee** and **thou** had yet to fall out of everyday use, and spelling was still subject to whim, but the language as a whole is recognizable and largely intelligible.

From the earliest times English has adopted words from other languages. Greek and Latin have contributed thousands of words and word-forming elements, either directly or via other European languages such as French, Spanish, Italian, and Portuguese. Traders and empire-builders brought back words from all corners and languages of the world: **coffee** from Turkey, **bungalow** and **jodhpurs** from India, **taboo** from Tonga; the list is endless. This process has never stopped; anyone having a **lager** and a **lasagne** at the **pub** on **karaoke** night is directly or indirectly 'borrowing' from four languages, more if he fancies a **whisky**, a **gin**, or a **vodka** and **lime**. Altogether over 1,000 languages have contributed to modern English.

Much of our everyday word-hoard comes from Old English: names for things such as ***house****,* ***book****,* ***clothes****, and* ***food****, of things we do such as* ***loving****,* ***working****,* ***reading****,* ***driving****,* ***eating****,* ***drinking****, even* ***living*** *itself, and all the handy little words like* ***a****,* ***the****,* ***how****,* ***why****,* ***when****,* ***where****,* ***I****,* ***you****,* ***and****,* ***but****,* ***to****,* ***for****,* ***in****,* ***out****,* ***with****,* ***be****,* ***have****,* ***do****, that help us put words together in strings to say or write our thoughts. Up until* ***now****, this paragraph has been written using only words of Old English origin.*

A large proportion of the words known to have existed in Old English survive in some form, if only in dialect, in place-names, or as part of a compound word:

Q Where does the bird-name REDSTART come from? I suppose 'red' refers to the bird's reddish tail-feathers. Does 'start' suggest that these are particularly noticeable when the bird moves, as when it is given a start?

Start has nothing to do with the bird being startled. **Redstart** is one of the few surviving remnants of Old English *steort*, which developed several meanings. One was the tail of an animal, which explains 'redstart'. This sense also survives in the dialect expression *start naked*, replaced in Standard English by the euphemistic 'stark' naked. **Start** also meant the stalk of a fruit or the handle of something; the former is obsolete, the latter now only dialect. The sense of a point or something sticking out appears in the name of a promontory, **Start Point**, in Devon; applied specifically to the points on a stag's horn it is still current in Canadian English. The two senses of **start** in Standard English are 'the innermost part of the bucket of a waterwheel' and 'the shaft or lever of a horse-mill'—by their nature neither is in common use.

Q What is the origin of the word WEREWOLF? What is, or was, a 'were'?

Werewolf, a being able to change from a person into a wolf, comes from late Old English. The first element is probably Old English *wer* 'a man'. The term more or less fell out of use after the 17th century as the belief in such creatures waned. It was revived in the 19th century by anthropologists and students of folklore, who also use **were** in the names of other legendary man-beasts, such as **were-bear, were-leopard**, and **were-jaguar**.

Wer also survives in the word **wergeld**, now used mainly by historians. In Germanic and Anglo-Saxon law this was the price assigned to a man according to his rank, payable as a fine or compensation by any person guilty of his murder; it was also sometimes exacted for other crimes. The word (spelt **weregild**) was also used by J. R. R. Tolkien in *The Lord of the Rings*, and has become part of the vocabulary of fantasy-writers.

Q What is the origin of NICKNAME? Is it in some way connected with Old Nick, the 'nickname' of the devil?

A nickname was originally an *eke-name*. In this context *eke* is an obsolete word from Old English *eaca*, meaning an addition or supplement, so that an *eke-name* was an additional name. In speech the *n* from 'an' eventually became transferred to the following word, giving the present-day form **nickname**. The same thing happened to the word **newt** (Middle English *ewt*, a variant spelling of **eft**, which remains a dialect word for newt), and the exact opposite to **adder** (*nædre* in Old English) and **apron** (Middle English *naperon*). As far as we know there is no connection with Old Nick, and how he got this *eke-name* is a mystery in itself.

---

*The **Oxford English Dictionary** sets out the etymologies of words in detail, where these are known. Where the word has changed its meaning in English the dictionaries on historical principles, the **OED** and the **New Shorter Oxford English Dictionary**, are able to show the development and make the derivation clear. In dictionaries of modern English it may be quite difficult to relate a word to its ancestor, or one sense of a word to another, if the 'link' is unfamiliar or obsolete.*

Q Where do we get the word BOOT from, as in the boot of a car? Could it be from French *boîte*, a box (like the American 'trunk', which obviously comes from a cabin trunk)? Come to think of it, what's the connection between the trunk of a tree and a cabin trunk—or an elephant's trunk, for that matter?

Boot as the luggage compartment of a car is a development in meaning from the 'footwear' sense. In the early 17th century boot meant 'the fixed external step of a coach' (the French had a similar term, *botte de carosse*), or an uncovered space on or by the step where the attendants sat. Later it meant a low outside compartment for servants or other 'inferior' passengers, at the front of or behind the main body of the vehicle. It then came to refer to the space under the seat of the driver or guard, used for luggage, and hence to the luggage compartment of a car.

Trunk is a word that has developed in several directions related to different aspects of its original meaning, the trunk of a tree. The sense of 'the main part' gave rise to 'the torso, the body not including the head and limbs' and to **trunk road** and **trunk call** (a telephone call using a *trunk line*, which connected two exchanges, rather than a call using lines both connected to the same exchange), as well as other lesser-known senses such as the shaft of a column and the case of a grandfather clock. The material gave rise to 'a wooden box or chest', originally made from a tree trunk, and thence a cabin trunk and the luggage compartment of a car. The shape gave us 'a cylindrical case for carrying or discharging explosives, such as the barrel of a mortar', a pipe used as a speaking tube, a pea-shooter, and an elephant's trunk.

Q Did the word TORY, now used of the British Conservative party, really once mean an Irish outlaw?

Yes, it is strange but true that the word was originally applied in the 17th century to the dispossessed Irish who lived as outlaws under English rule, and it probably comes from the Irish *toraidhe* 'outlaw, fugitive' (from *toiṙ* 'pursue'). It became for a time quite widely used for outlaws and rebels of any description, and during the political turmoil of around 1680 'Tory' was given as an insulting nickname to those who supported James, Duke of York (James II) as heir to the throne. The opposing party, who wished to exclude James as heir because of his Roman Catholicism, were nicknamed 'Whig', which had previously been a term of abuse for Scottish Presbyterian rebels. As often happens, the 'insults' were adopted by those who bore them: **Quaker** and **Methodist** began similarly as disparaging nicknames.

During the 18th century the labels 'Tory' and 'Whig' were used for the two main political factions, the Tories being broadly associated with the Established Church of England and the country gentry, and the Whigs with the religious dissenters and the rising industrial classes. The early 19th century saw the establishment of the Conservative party, to which the term 'Tory' has remained informally attached. The reforming tradition of the Whigs was inherited by the Liberal party, but the term 'Whig' has largely fallen out of political use.

Q My *Concise Oxford Dictionary* says that the word TAWDRY comes from 'St Audrey's lace'—can you tell me more about this, please?

A *St Audrey's lace* was a type of fine silk scarf or ribbon worn by women, usually around the neck, and very fashionable in the 16th and early 17th centuries. The term was later shortened to *tawdry lace*. The name Audrey is itself an adaptation, via Norman French, of Old English *Æðelðryð* or *Etheldreda*; St Etheldreda was a 7th-century Saxon princess who founded and presided over a great religious house at Ely, on the site now occupied by the cathedral. Tawdry laces were traditionally sold at the fair held at Ely on her feast day, 17 October. They were a very acceptable gift from a gentleman to his lady; no doubt cheap imitations were produced for the labourer to buy for his lass, which led to the association with flashy, poor-quality finery. Etheldreda is said to have died of cancer of the throat, which she believed was a punishment for wearing showy necklaces in her youth. Perhaps she would have regarded the fall of the tawdry lace from a high-fashion item to an object of contempt as another example of pride going before a fall.

The much less common word **tantony** has a similar history. St Antony was a 3rd-century saint, living in Egypt, and is regarded as the founder of monasticism. He is usually depicted with his emblems, which include a bell and a pig. 'Tantony' came to be used for a small church-bell or hand-bell, and for the smallest pig in a litter. To follow someone 'like a tantony pig' was to traipse around after them obsequiously, to be always under their feet in the hope of attention or reward. St Antony's name was also given to the disease now known as erysipelas and to ergot-poisoning, both once known as *St Antony's fire*, as it was believed that a visit to his shrine would bring about a cure. *St Vitus's dance*, the old name of Sydenham's chorea, has a similar derivation.

By all accounts Etheldreda and Antony were wise, pious, and widely revered, while poor Vitus was an innocent child martyred with his family, and it seems a pity that their names should be remembered in such ways. Other saints have been more fortunate: St Bernard of Menthon (923–1008) for the breed of dog raised and trained by the monks of his Alpine hospice to rescue travellers lost in the snow; St Benedict (*c.*480–*c.*547) for the liqueur **Benedictine**, first made at the Benedictine monastery at Fécamp in northern France; and St Philibert, a 7th-century abbot, for the **filberts** gathered on his feast day (20 August). **St Luke's Summer** and **St Martin's Summer** both refer to periods of unseasonably warm weather around their feast days, in October and November respectively, while many saints have flowers named after them. Examples will be found under the entry for *saint* in the *OED*.

Q The word TYRE originally applied to the iron hoop which binds the wooden section of a cartwheel, but the dictionary derivation from 'attire' seems far-fetched. Doesn't it just refer to the band 'tying' the wheel together?

The derivation of **tyre** from **attire** 'clothing' may seem rather peculiar, but accords better with the historical evidence. The word **tier** 'a thing which ties' is unknown in English before the 1660s, and was always spelt *tier* or *tyer*. The word for the covering of a wheel, however, dates back to the late 1400s, and was spelt *tire* or *tyre*, but never with an *-er*, which would be expected if it was originally a 'tie-er'. It did not originally apply to a single band of metal, but was a collective term for a set of separate pieces known individually as **strakes**.

Although 'attire' is now rather an archaic or poetic word for clothing, it was more commonly used in past centuries, and also had the more general sense of 'equipment'. The view of the covering of the wheel as clothing is also perhaps reflected in the fact that the action of fitting tyres was called 'shoeing' and an iron-bound wheel is described as 'shod'.

Q Can you tell me the origin of 'know A from a ball's foot'? I came across it in a book the other day, and I seem to remember a similar phrase concerning a bull's foot.

The oldest version of the phrase that we know of dates from about 1400: *I knew not an A from the wyndmylne* (windmill), *ne a B from a bole* (bull) *foot*. It meant that the person was completely illiterate, not knowing the shape of the letters from something vaguely resembling them—the sails of a windmill or the cloven hoofprint of a bull. The phrase remained in use for many years, usually just as *did not know B from a bull's foot*. However, the version that has come down to us is the apparently nonsensical *not know A from a bull's foot*, and it has come to mean ignorant rather than illiterate: *I don't know A from a bull's foot about cricket*. The variation 'ball's foot' shows how easily such a phrase can change once the image of the bull's hoofprint has been lost.

Q Where do we get '£', the pound sign, from?

The symbol is simply a capital L, written in copperplate, with one or two crossbars. Such bars over or through letters were formerly in frequent use to indicate an abbreviation, or to show that certain letters have been omitted. The L stood for the Latin word *libra*, a Roman unit of weight, which also gives rise to the abbreviation **lb**. for a pound in weight. The linking of currency and weight reflects the fact that originally the pound sterling had the value of a pound weight of sterling silver.

Q Where does the term 'the curate's egg', for something having both good and bad qualities, come from?

TRUE HUMILITY.

Right Reverend Host. "I'm afraid you've got a bad Egg, Mr. Jones!"
The Curate. "Oh no, my Lord, I assure you! Parts of it are excellent!"

The phrase is derived from this cartoon which appeared in *Punch* in November 1895. The joke is, of course, that a bad egg is wholly repulsive (as anyone who has smelt one will know). A *Punch* cartoon of 1918 showed Lloyd George carrying an Easter egg labelled *Draft Peace Terms*, with the caption 'I don't say it's a perfect egg, but parts of it, as the saying is, are excellent'; this suggests that the phrase was well established and moving towards its modern usage.

The original cartoon is one of a number which appeared in *Punch* in the 19th and early 20th centuries, depicting the lower ranks of the clergy as impoverished, down-trodden, and very much dependent on patronage and even hand-outs from richer members of the community. In this case the bishop is obviously far from poor; the curate, at the bottom of the clerical heap and no doubt hoping for advancement, dare not offend.

Q I looked up AMPERSAND in the *Concise Oxford Dictionary*, where it says that it's a corruption of '*and per se*

***and*' ('&' by itself is 'and'). I can see how 'and per se and' becomes 'ampersand', but how did the phrase itself come into being?**

The ampersand (&) is a kind of shorthand contraction of Latin *et* (= and). The symbol was added to the end of the written alphabet, as one of the characters that a medieval scribe had to learn. In later centuries children reciting the alphabet would chant '. . . x, y, z, and *per se* and' (*per se* being Latin for 'by itself'), meaning 'the symbol & by itself represents and'. It seems quite likely that they had no idea of the meaning, and simply repeated 'x, y, z, ampersand', believing this to be the name of the symbol. The first written record we have of **ampersand** actually used as the name comes from the mid-19th century, but variations of it, such as *ampusand*, *ampassy*, and *ampussy*, appear in dialect dictionaries, suggesting that it was already used in spoken English.

Q What is the origin of the term LOVE used instead of 'nil' when scoring in tennis?

It seems to have been adapted from the phrase 'to play for love', meaning 'to play for the love of the game', i.e. without stakes, for nothing. It is probably not a corruption of the French *l'œuf* 'an egg' (from the resemblance between an egg and a nought), though this suggestion is often made. Eggs do have their place in cricket: the phrase 'out for a duck', meaning 'out without scoring', is said to be short for 'out for a duck's egg', the duck's egg being the large nought recorded on the scoreboard.

The French are apparently not responsible for 'love' in tennis. In fact, most other nations are innocent of charges brought against them by the English language.

Q What is the origin of FRENCH LEAVE, meaning absence without permission. Surely the French army has rules about leave?

The phrase **to take French leave** has nothing to do with soldiers going AWOL. It dates from the middle of the 18th century, and is supposed to derive from the French custom at that time of leaving a ball or dinner without saying goodbye to the host or hostess. However, the French version of the saying is *s'en aller* or *filer à l'anglaise*. At the time it is first recorded Britain had recently emerged from the Seven Years War, in which the British, Prussians, and Hanoverians were allied against the Russians, French, and some other nations, and it is interesting to see that, while French and Russian attribute such bad manners to the English, German, like English, blames the French.

It seems likely that this is just another of the many English slang terms that refer disparagingly to the French—**pardon my French** to apologize for swearing, **French letter** for condom, **French postcards** with pictures of naked ladies (the French called them *American postcards*), and any number of terms, now obsolete, for sexually transmitted diseases. The only other nationality to have attracted so much unfavourable attention is the Dutch, with **Dutch courage** inspired by alcohol, **Dutch treat** (or **going Dutch**) when one pays for oneself, and **double Dutch** for unintelligible or nonsensical language. Earlier terms included *Dutch consolation* ('Cheer up, it could be worse') and *Dutch feast* (at which the host drank more than his guests).

Most languages contain such sayings concerning other nations. The fact that English has so many involving the French and Dutch no doubt reflects the fact that they are Britain's closest neighbours as well as having been, from time to time, its enemies.

Q In his humorous book *How to be an Alien*, George Mikes suggests that the use of animal names such as PIG as

terms of abuse is an un-English introduction from continental Europe. Is this true?

The use of animal names as terms of abuse is probably a very long-standing feature of most languages, including English. The introduction to the *Dictionary of Invective* by Hugh Rawson (1989) remarks that 'very few animal names have not been used as epithets at one time or another'. Of the animal names used to describe humans or human characteristics (with various degrees of abusiveness), some are known to date back many centuries—the Psalmist called himself a worm (Psalms 22: 6), and Jesus of Nazareth is reported to have called King Herod 'that fox' (Luke 13: 32). The *OED*'s first recorded dates for some of them (in English) are given below:

> **worm** *c.*825 (in an Anglo-Saxon version of the Psalms); **fox** *c.*1000 (in an Anglo-Saxon version of Luke's gospel); **hound** *c.*1000; **cat** *by* 1225; **ape** *c.*1230 (meaning 'a mimic'); **dog** *c.*1325; **bitch** *c.*1400; **baboon** *c.*1500; **sow** 1508; **pig** 1546; **toad** *by* 1568; **vixen** 1575; **ass** 1578; **monkey** 1589; **snake** 1590; **nag** 1598; **cow** 1696 (but from 1581 meaning 'coward'); **donkey** 1840 (the animal name itself only dates from the late 18th century).

There seems to be a fair balance of the sexes, and some words such as **cat** and **sow**, now more often specific, were applied indiscriminately to men and women. Few of the above words are recorded back into the Anglo-Saxon period, so it might be possible to blame Norse, Danish, Norman, and other immigrants for some of the later terms. Certainly *bikkja* 'bitch' was used as a term of abuse in Old Norse (surviving in modern Icelandic, especially directed towards bad horses!), and the expression *kattar sonr* 'son of a cat' in some contexts meant 'bastard'. However, the early written records do not adequately represent colloquial usage in Old English.

Oddly, though, Mikes may well be right in the case of **pig**, which is recorded from 1546 but remained very rare until the late 19th century, and could well have arisen in imitation of the French use of *cochon*.

It is clear from the historical evidence that the respectability of such terms may change quite considerably. The 19th-century editor of the *OED* entry for **ass** noted that the word was 'now disused in polite literature and speech', though it was used casually enough earlier that century, and again early this century. Similarly at **bitch** it is noted 'not now in decent use; but formerly common in literature': indeed, Hobbes's 1675 translation of Homer's *Odyssey* contains the line:

Ulysses looking sourly answered, You Bitch.

This would have been quite unthinkable in the 19th century. It is interesting to note that in modern colloquial use **son of a bitch** often achieves a mildness almost approaching that of **bloke**.

It is not only ancient words that interest our correspondents. Thousands of new expressions and phrases are added to the language every year, keeping our New Words team constantly busy, and they give rise to a number of enquiries. Sometimes, however, they are not as 'new' as they seem—they have just been away for a while.

Q Recently I have seen the word FEISTY used a lot; it seems to be applied to rather tough career-women and to be almost a term of approval. Is it an Americanism?

Feisty itself came to Britain from the USA. It was originally a dialect word meaning 'aggressive, excitable, touchy', and could be used of any person or animal. Quotations in the *OED* refer to a feisty mare who 'jumped straight upwards and broke the tongue outen the plow' and to a man getting a little feisty and argumentative after a few drinks. A quotation from the late 1960s seems to be getting closer to the modern use which you have noted: 'He couldn't shake her loose—she hung onto his arm, feisty as a terrier' (from J. Potts, *Trash Stealer*).

This quotation also takes us nearer to the word's origin. Feisty comes from a variant spelling of *fist*—not the closed hand, but an unrelated Middle English word meaning 'to break wind' or 'the act of breaking wind'. In the 16th century *fisting hound* or *cur* was a term of abuse for a pampered pet dog. This died out in British English, but in the USA it became shortened to *fist* or *feist*, and was used for a small mongrel or terrier—hence 'feisty', with the primary meanings of aggressiveness and touchiness, but also with implications of assertiveness, tenacity, and the ability to take care of oneself.

Q My children have recently taken to using the term 'dob someone in' for what we always used to call 'telling tales'. They seem to have got it from one of the Australian soaps they are forever watching. The eldest informs me that it must be English because it's in one of your dictionaries. Where does it come from?

Dob someone in, meaning 'to inform against, to implicate, to betray', is certainly English, although not, at present, British English. It appears in the *Australian Pocket Oxford Dictionary* and the *OED* itself, of course, and in others including the *New Shorter Oxford English Dictionary* and the *Concise Oxford Dictionary*. In each case it is clearly labelled as Australian. However, **dob** itself is a variant form of **dab**, with the meaning 'to put or throw down carelessly'. **Dob** is recorded in the dialects of several English counties, so the phrase has British English ancestry. Other Antipodean terms with similar backgrounds are **dag** and **daggy**, now used of people or clothes which are out of style, but probably related to the 'dags' of muck-encrusted wool on a sheep's back end, recorded in Kentish dialect; **dill** 'a stupid person', related to **dilly**, a West Country dialect word meaning foolish; and **dunny**, an outside lavatory or earth-closet, short for *dunnaken*, found in dictionaries of 18th-century underworld slang and possibly 'transported' to the penal colonies. It remains to be seen whether these will be accepted into British English, as **soap** has been (originally US **soap opera**, as this kind of programme was often sponsored by manufacturers of washing-powders), or whether these 'long-lost cousins' are only visiting.

During this century, and particularly since World War II, events on the world stage have put many words and phrases into English. Some, like ***Iron Curtain****,* ***perestroika****, and* ***apartheid****, are already being overtaken by events and will soon be labelled as historical, belonging to one particular time and place. Others seem likely to become permanent features of the language, being applied to other events and circumstances than the ones that gave rise to them.*

Q Whenever there's any sort of political scandal, sooner or later someone calls it something-*gate*. I remember the Watergate scandal in the 1970s, but where did this get its name from? Who or what was the WATERGATE?

Watergate was the name of the building in Washington, DC, which housed the national headquarters of the Democratic Party. In 1972 it was revealed that the building had been bugged, the Party headquarters had been burgled, and confidential papers had been taken or copied. Senior members of the Republican administration were implicated and the resulting scandal led to the resignation of the President, Richard M. Nixon. Even before this affair was fully over, journalists began using **-gate** as a word-forming element indicating some form of scandal, tacked on to the name of the place where it occurred, the name of a person or organization, or a commodity or activity involved. The individual scandals often fade from the public mind quite quickly but the suffix itself goes on. It is looking rather hackneyed of late, but we suspect that its usefulness as a shorthand device for headline writers will preserve it. Provided, of course, that our politicians and journalists can keep up a steady supply of real or imagined scandals.

Occasionally our correspondents write to us while our own investigations are under way, as in the case of this enquiry, which found our lexicographer part-way through the process of research:

Q I assume that the phrase ETHNIC CLEANSING is a translation from Serbo-Croat, but was it first used in this conflict, or is it older?

I have been preparing a provisional entry for **ethnic cleansing** for the third edition of the *Oxford English Dictionary* and am awaiting a reply to a letter I wrote to one of our consultants. In the meantime I will tell you what we know.

Our department has access to the NEXIS electronic database, and this was searched in order to find the earliest possible citation. From this it seems that the term was coined during the present Yugoslavian conflict; our first citation was from the *Washington Post* of 2 August 1991. It therefore seems likely that **ethnic cleansing** is a translation of a phrase used by one of the parties involved.

Some weeks later . . .

Further to my recent letter, I can now pass on some further information which our consultant has supplied to us.

The Serbo-Croat equivalent of the term is *etničko čišćenje*. This particular phrase appears to be modern, but the word *čišćenje* was used as a euphemism in the phrase *čišćenje terena* 'cleansing of the territory' by the Ustashi (supporters of Croatian nationalism and separatism holding power in Croatia in 1941–5). Apparently the term 'ethnic cleansing' may have been used first by the Belgian press, in which case the Serbo-Croat *etničko čišćenje* would itself be a translation from French or Flemish. However, I fear that the current situation makes it impossible to verify this information.

Sometimes, of course, we cannot supply an etymology; we simply do not know, or there is no documentary evidence to support or refute a conjecture. This is particularly so in the case of words or phrases that are, or were originally, dialect, colloquial, or slang. Such words may have been in spoken use for many years before being written down; subject to who-knows-what changes in pronunciation and meaning as they passed from mouth to mouth. Frustrated readers are left with tantalizing phrases such as 'origin uncertain', 'perhaps from', 'perhaps related to', etc. However, we would rather be 'honest doubters' than present as fact a derivation we are not sure of.

Q Your dictionary says that TWIG comes from Old English, but that the origin of 'twig' meaning to catch on or understand is unknown. How can this be?

The noun **twig**, a small branch, comes from Old English *twigge*. As for the verb, we don't really know, and we think it may not be related to the noun at all. Some people believe it comes from Gaelic; Irish and Scottish Gaelic *tuig* 'to understand' may be connected in some way, and *to twig* has certainly had both these meanings. It is possible that even if the word does not come from Gaelic its use may have been popularized by Scottish or Irish speakers of English who were also familiar with the Gaelic words, but we have no firm evidence that it originated in an area that would make this likely.

Q My *Concise Oxford Dictionary* gives the etymology of BOGUS as 'US, orig. unknown', but another dictionary I have says that it comes from a word for a machine for making counterfeit coins. Who's right?

Both are, but we would claim that we were more right! The earliest evidence we have for **bogus** is as a noun referring to a machine for making counterfeit coins, or to such a coin; quotations for it as an adjective to describe something false appear later. So your other dictionary is probably right in saying that the adjective comes from the noun. However, what we do not know, and what your other dictionary does not deal with, is why such a machine was called a bogus. The first quotation in the *OED* is dated 1827, from the *Painesville* (*Ohio*) *Telegraph*: it was sent to the Dictionary by Dr S. Willard of Chicago. The *OED* tells the story as Dr Willard supplied it: 'Mr Eber D. Howe, who was then editor of that paper, describes in his *Autobiography* (1878) the discovery of such a piece of mechanism in the hands of a gang of coiners in Painesville in May 1827; it was a mysterious-looking object, and someone in the crowd styled it a "bogus"; a designation adopted in succeeding numbers of the paper.' Dr Willard considered this to have been short for *tantrabogus*, a word familiar to him from his childhood, and which in his father's time was commonly applied in Vermont to any strange-looking object. Dr Willard also pointed out that 'tantarrabob' was a Devonshire dialect word for the devil (see p. 117). **Bogus** may therefore be related to the group which includes **bugbear** and the **bogeyman**, but as we do not know the ultimate origin of these terms this leaves us very little wiser.

Q What is the origin of the phrase TO RAIN CATS AND DOGS?

No one really knows. One theory is that it is associated with the Greek word *katadoupoi*, meaning a cataract. Another links it to Norse folklore, in which cats were supposed to be able to influence the weather and dogs were associated with storms. A third is that, in the days when street drainage was very inefficient (where it existed at all), small animals caught in a downpour might easily drown; after the rain their bodies would be found lying around as though they had fallen from the sky.

The phrase is first recorded in 1738, used by Jonathan Swift, but almost a century earlier Richard Brome had used the expression '*rain dogs and polecats*' in his play *The City Witt*. If this was the original version then none of the above theories really hold water, if you'll forgive the pun. However, Brome may have been using a humorous variant of a phrase already familiar to him and his audience.

Q I've been trying to find the origin of JACOB'S JOIN, a phrase well known in Lancashire in my youth, meaning a communal meal or party to which everyone contributes some food. It does not appear in any dictionary, as far as I know. Can you help?

The term **Jacob's join** is new to us; it does not appear in dialect dictionaries and we have no examples of it. We therefore cannot give you an authoritative derivation, but we can hazard a guess. **Join** is found in various dialects referring to different kinds of communal activity, from sharing work to pooling resources to buy drink. We wonder if Jacob might be the biblical figure, the father of Joseph who had the coat of many colours and who was sold into slavery by his envious brothers. Genesis 42–3 tells the story of Jacob sending his sons to buy corn in Egypt, where they meet Joseph, who has become Pharaoh's steward. They do not recognize him, although he knows them. On a second visit Jacob tells them to take the steward a present 'of the best fruits in the land . . . and a little honey, spices, and myrrh, nuts and almonds'. The brothers take these to Joseph's house, where they all eat together, Joseph providing the rest of the meal. The story of Joseph and his brothers is one of the better-known episodes of the Old Testament, and this detail seems to us to supply a plausible explanation of the term although, owing to the complete lack of evidence, we cannot promise that it is the right one.

There are a number of words whose origins are known, it would seem, to everyone except us. Barely a week goes by without someone writing in with the well-known tale of how one or other of them came into being. While we do appreciate our readers' interest and concern, we are usually aware of the stories. In many cases there are objections to them, often concerning dating. In any case, unless we have proof—which in the nature of things is often impossible—we still have to say 'origin unknown', even if we think there may be an element of truth in the tale. We list below some of the better-known and more persistent stories in the hope that we can save some potential correspondents the trouble of writing.

Q ABOMINABLE

We do know the derivation of this word—it comes via Old French from Latin, ultimately from *ab* 'off, away, from' and *omen, omin-* 'a prophetic sign'. We include it here because there is a very long-standing misapprehension about its origin which we still occasionally hear. It was once widely believed to be from *ab* + *homine* (from *homo* 'human being'), and was spelt *abhominable* in medieval Latin, Old French, and in English until well into the 17th century; it is spelt this way in the first folio of Shakespeare.

This misapprehension has affected the word's usage. Its primary meaning is 'loathsome, detestable, disgusting'; more loosely 'very unpleasant', but it has had implications of inhumanity or bestial, perverted humanity, rather than of bad omen as the true derivation would suggest. When Hamlet speaks of bad actors who 'imitated humanity so abominably' the pun is no doubt intentional, and this feeling of a beast resembling a man may be behind the term **abominable snowman** for the mythical yeti.

Q BUG

From one of the oldest spurious etymologies to one of the latest. A **bug** is a hidden fault in a system which must be found and removed before the system will work. Computer programmers can often spend more time 'debugging' a program than writing it in the first place. The story goes that some hapless insect crept into an early electromechanical computer and became squashed between the contacts of a relay, causing the machine to fail. When the poor creature was found the incident was written up in the system log-book and the term **bug** subsequently spread throughout the computer industry. According to some versions of the tale, the log-book (with the bug neatly taped to the page) is still in existence.

The first examples we have of **bug** being used in this sense date from the mid-20th century, but an earlier example, from the 1880s, refers to Edison searching for a 'bug' in his phonograph; the quotation makes it clear that it is an imaginary rather than an actual insect. No doubt machines have broken down because of insects in the works, and perhaps this did give rise to the term, but it seems to have spread from engineering to computers rather than originating in the computer industry. The word **bug** was once used for a hobgoblin or bogeyman, but this usage was obsolete long before computers were invented; they are, however, sometimes attacked by a near-relative, the gremlin.

Q CODSWALLOP

There are various theories concerning the origin of **codswallop**, meaning 'nonsense' or 'drivel'. Eric Partridge, in his *Dictionary of Slang and Unconventional English*, suggests that the word may have referred to the testicles of the cod, as very tiny objects worthy of contempt. The most popular theory, which appears in *Brewer's Dictionary of Phrase and Fable*, is as follows: in 1875 a Mr Hiram Codd patented a bottle with a marble in the neck for mineral water or other fizzy drinks. The pressure of gas in the liquid kept the marble firmly in the neck of the bottle until it was pressed inwards to enable the liquid to be poured. **Wallop** was a slang term for beer, and *Codd's wallop* came to be used by beer drinkers as a derisive term for weak or gassy beer, or for soft drinks.

Two things go against this theory: one is that **codswallop** is not recorded until the mid-20th century, rather a long time after Mr Codd's invention; the other is that we know of no examples of *Codd's wallop*, which might be expected as an early form. Neither objection is conclusive. Slang terms can take a long time to get into the written language (**codswallop** was certainly known to one of our editors at least five years before its first citation in the *OED*, and it may be considerably older) and it is possible that the connection with Codd's bottle had been forgotten by the time the word was first written down.

However, these objections do shed considerable doubt, and it is safer to regard this as a colourful story rather than a serious explanation.

Q GAY

Since the 1960s homosexual men, and to a lesser extent women, have used **gay** to refer to themselves and their sexuality in a positive way, and many people believe that it stands for 'good as you'. In fact the term has been used to mean homosexual, or with implications of homosexuality, at least since the 1930s, and perhaps for much longer.

From the middle of the 17th century a **gay man** or a **gay dog** was a man-about-town, leading a social life varying from active and merry to downright dissolute, and in the 19th century **gay** was used of prostitutes—women being judged by different standards. There is a document from the late 19th century concerning a male prostitute, in which it is impossible to say for sure whether **gay** refers to his sexuality or his livelihood. In American slang of the late 19th century a *gay cat* was a young hobo, particularly one who went around with an older man; a quotation from Raymond Chandler says that 'there is always a connotation of homosexuality'. This quotation dates from 1950, when **gay** for homosexual was already well established (although not widely known); an American slang dictionary of 1935 lists *geycat* as a homosexual boy.

Homosexuals who wished to declare their sexuality in a

positive way therefore had a word already in their vocabulary which was short and non-clinical, and which to the world at large meant 'happy', with overtones of celebration and pride. 'Good as you' was fortuitous.

Q LOO

There are several well-known theories about the origin of **loo** for a lavatory. The 'favourite' in terms of the number of times it is suggested is the cry of 'gardyloo' (from the French *regardez l'eau* 'watch out for the water') shouted by considerate servants in medieval times when emptying a chamber-pot into the street. As this expression seems to have disappeared in the mid-19th century, and **loo** did not emerge until some way into this century, the connection is problematical. Another suggestion based on French, that *le lieu* 'the place' was used as a Victorian euphemism, is also unsupported by evidence.

A third suggestion, noted by some of our correspondents, refers to the iron cisterns found in many outhouses in the early part of this century, and bearing the trade name **Waterloo**. This is more credible in terms of the dates, but evidence is still elusive, and we cannot reach any firm conclusion.

Q OK

Again, there are several suggestions for this one, including: via Black American English from words in various West African languages meaning 'all right, yes indeed' etc.; Choctaw *oke* or *okeh* 'it is so'; Greek *ola kala* 'it is good'; Scots *och aye* 'oh yes'; French *aux Cayes* 'from Cayes'—a port in Haiti well known for the quality of its rum; the initials of *Obediah Kelly*, a railway freight agent who initialled lading documents he had checked.

The one best supported by documentary evidence is that it comes from *orl korrekt* 'all correct'—one of a number of similar humorous misspellings which went through a brief period of popularity in the late 1830s. In the 1840 presidential elections **O.K.** was adopted as an election slogan by supporters of the Democratic candidate Martin Van Buren, who was born in Kinderhook in New York State. He was nicknamed 'Old Kinderhook' and his supporters formed the *Old Kinderhook*, or *OK*, *Club*. The term caught on almost immediately in the USA, although it was not common in Britain until the early 20th century.

A personal favourite among all the theories we have been sent is that **OK** comes from **kayo** (from K.O.) meaning 'knock-out'—if a boxer had not been kayoed he was O.K. Unfortunately this is easily disproved by the dates; the first date for **kayo** is more than 80 years later than **OK**.

Q PENGUIN

The theory that **penguin** comes from Welsh or Cornish *penn-gwynn* 'white head', or from a related Breton word, has a long history. It was assumed by several writers in the 16th and 17th centuries, and is naturally favoured by Celts.

The name **penguin** was first applied to the great auk of Newfoundland (now extinct), which did not have a conspicuously white head, although it had a patch of white behind the bill. The modern Breton name for the bird is quite different. Another possibility is that these birds were originally called *pin-wing*, from their flipper-like wings, which would apply equally well to the birds we now know as penguins. The old local pronunciation in Newfoundland is said to have been 'pin-wing', which is at least suggestive.

A connection with Latin *pinguis* 'fat' has been proposed, but this seems too scholarly a word to be a likely source, although it may have influenced the spelling of the great auk's scientific name, *Pinguinus*.

Q POSH

This is probably the best known of all the spurious etymologies. On the voyage between the British Isles and the Indian subcontinent, cabins on the side away from the sun—the port side going out, and the starboard side coming back—were cooler and more desirable, and therefore more expensive. The well-to-do travelled 'port out, starboard home', the initials 'P.O.S.H.' being written on documents to show this, and the word **posh** came to mean smart, stylish, socially superior, or with upper-class pretensions.

The immediate objections to this derivation are similar to those affecting **codswallop**. The story did not begin to circulate until the 1930s, when the word had already been in use for twenty years or so, and there are no examples of **posh** written in any way that suggests an acronym. George Chowdharay-Best, an experienced and indefatigable researcher who has been a major contributor to the Dictionary Department's work for many years, has carried out a thorough investigation of this and other theories. Despite examining shipping company documents and consulting regular travellers, he found no evidence to support the story. An account of his investigations, too long to reproduce here, was published in *Mariner's Mirror*, January 1971.

Q QUIZ

The story goes that Richard Daly, the proprietor of a theatre in Dublin, made a bet that within forty-eight hours a nonsense word could be made known throughout the city, and that the public would give a meaning to it. After the evening performance he gave out cards with **quiz** written on them to members of the theatre staff, telling them to write the word up on walls all over Dublin. The next day the whole city was buzzing with this strange new word which had appeared overnight, and within a short time it had become part of the language.

Certainly **quiz** is a very odd word, with no obvious derivation or relationship to any other word, and it is very tempting to believe the tale. Unfortunately the most detailed account gives the date of Mr Daly's exploit as 21 August 1791 and the word itself was first recorded nine years earlier, used to mean an odd or eccentric person. To **quiz** someone was to make fun of them, and a **quiz** came to mean a practical joke or a witticism. This set of meanings is now rare, except for the derivative **quizzical**.

In the mid-19th century, the word **quiz** emerged in dialect with the meaning 'to question or interrogate'. In the USA it meant specifically to question students on their work; the noun arose some twenty years later, meaning 'an act of questioning, an oral examination, the questions set', and this developed into the sort of question-and-answer entertainment we know today. Again, the word's origin is a mystery; it may be a transferred use of the existing **quiz**, perhaps influenced by the word **inquisitive**, but we cannot be sure, and in our historical dictionaries we prefer to treat the two sets of meanings as belonging to two distinct word-groups. This more modern sense of **quiz** would appear to be separated by too much time and distance to be Mr Daly's word.

Q SNOB

We probably get more letters about **snob** than any other of our 'orphan' words. All our correspondents agree that it comes from an abbreviation of the Latin phrase *sine nobilitate* 'without nobility', used to distinguish those of humble birth from their betters. The circumstances in which this phrase was allegedly used vary: added after the names in lists of Oxford or Cambridge students in various centuries, giving rise to the 'snobs' table' or 'snobs' entrance' which these poor scholars had to use; as a marginal note in Polish genealogies of the 18th century; on lists of ship's passengers (to make sure that no one unsuitable dined at the captain's table); and on lists of invited guests to reassure the servants that the person had no title and they would not find themselves without a job (or a head, depending on the century) by announcing or addressing him accordingly.

Snob (or *snab* in Scotland) is first recorded in the late 18th century, meaning a shoemaker or shoemaker's apprentice. It was used by Cambridge students at about this time for anyone not a member of the university; a 'townsman' as opposed to a 'gownsman'—there are no examples of it being used to designate a poor or untitled student. In the early 19th century it was used for a person with no 'breeding'; both the 'honest snob' who knew his place and had no pretensions to gentility and the vulgar or ostentatious person forever showing off and aping his 'betters'. At this time it was sometimes contrasted with **nob**, a member of the upper echelons of society. From here it developed its current meaning: a person who wishes to be associated with those he or she perceives as socially superior, and who patronizes or ignores those perceived as inferior in social position, education, or taste. Thackeray, in his *Book of Snobs*, has a comprehensive and delightful definition:

> You who despise your neighbour, are a Snob; you who forget your own friends, meanly to follow after those of a higher degree, are a Snob; you who are ashamed of your poverty, and blush for your calling, are a Snob; as are you who boast of your pedigree, or are proud of your wealth.

As for *sine nobilitate*, we are quite willing to believe that it was used at some time in one or more of the many contexts suggested, but we do not see why this would have given rise to a term for a shoemaker. The stories may be true; we doubt whether they are relevant.

Q WALLY

This is used as a term of mild abuse for a foolish, inept, or ineffectual man, or someone who is hopelessly out of step with current fashions in dress or behaviour but totally unaware of it. Many suggestions have been put forward: the name of Dennis the Menace's enemy, Walter, in *The Beano* comic; a Cockney term for a pickled gherkin; or a Scottish term for false teeth. **Wally** was also a Scottish term for a toy (surviving in the ornamental china dogs still known as **wally-dags**), and *wallydrag* or *wallydraigle* was once a dialect term for a weak or ineffectual person, although it was usually applied to women.

A story frequently told is that, at one of the large pop-music festivals of the 1960s, a person (or a dog) called Wally became separated from his companions. His name was announced several times over the public-address system, and taken up as a chant by the crowd at this and subsequent events. It would be fun if this were true, and the dates fit well enough, but we may never know for sure.

Q ZIT

Many people believe that the comedian Jasper Carrott invented the word **zit** for a pimple. During a television programme in the early 1970s he said that pimple was 'far too soft a word for the little monsters', and that zit would be a much better one. While agreeing that zit is much more graphic, we cannot give him the credit for inventing it, as we have quotations in the *OED* from the 1960s. We still do not know its origins, although it seems to have arisen in North American teenage slang. However, Mr Carrott may have introduced the word into British English and he certainly helped to popularize it.

3

What is the difference between . . . ?

One of the many subjects that interest our readers is varieties of English and the differences between them.

Q What is the difference between colloquial English, slang, and jargon?

Colloquial language and slang overlap to a certain extent. Both are informal, and are more common in spoken than in written language. You might use either when speaking or writing to a friend; when speaking to a person in authority or writing to an acquaintance you might use colloquial language but avoid slang, and you would not use either in a formal letter or report.

The difference between them lies mainly in who uses them, and why. Colloquial language is the language of informal everyday speech, and its words and phrases will be known and used naturally by most people having the language as their mother tongue.

Slang is more often used consciously, in particular circumstances or within a restricted group. Each generation of teenagers makes up its own slang and uses it as a private language. Most trades and professions have their own slang words, often shorter and simpler words for technical terms, which are used partly for convenience and partly to show that the speaker is 'in the trade' and 'in the know'. Slang can be quite vivid and picturesque, and may be used in fun or to shock. It can also be used to show that the user is speaking informally; that he or she feels at ease or is trying to put the listener at ease.

Colloquial terms tend to stay in the language for a long time and to be fairly stable. Slang, on the other hand, may die out fairly quickly or may escape from its restricted usage and be accepted into colloquial or standard English; **clever**, **fun**, and **mob** were all once regarded as slang. (This is less true of professional slang, where the 'in' group is stable although individual members of it come and go.)

Jargon refers to the language of a trade or profession, which may include the slang, used inappropriately. Technical language is perfectly all right when used between those who understand it. It becomes jargon when uttered to those who do not or cannot be expected to understand it, or when it seems to be used merely to impress rather than to communicate. Jargon can be used deliberately to gull the lay person, but is often the result of experts forgetting that their terminology needs explaining; computer instruction manuals are notorious examples.

Q In your dictionaries words are often labelled 'obs.', 'hist.', or 'arch.' I know all these terms refer to old words, but I'm not quite sure of the difference.

The abbreviations stand for **obsolete**, **historical**, and **archaic**. An **obsolete** word is one which is no longer used. A **historical** term refers to a thing that no longer exists, or is no longer used. For example, **wergeld** (see p. 9) is no longer part of the legal system, but a historian may wish to refer to it. The word **warming-pan** is also labelled *hist.*; warming-pans still exist but are no longer used and are not part of modern life (except hung on the wall of the lounge bar).

Archaic language is old-fashioned and no longer appears in everyday speech and writing, but is sometimes used to give an air of authenticity to a novel etc. set in the past. It can be very effective if not overdone, for example if the knight speaks more or less standard English but addresses the king as *Sire* rather than *Your Majesty*; but '*Zounds*,' *quoth he* on every other page rapidly becomes tiresome. I have seen archaic language used in children's computer games set in the past. This would seem to require a degree of linguistic awareness beyond a child's abilities, but those I have watched have no difficulty in interpreting the language, nor do they use the archaisms in their everyday speech; they seem to appreciate that the words are part of the game and not of the real world.

The language of former times can often be difficult for modern readers:

Q I have been reading the King James Bible, and I am confused about the difference between *-est* and *-eth*. Could you please explain why and how they are used?

Most languages have endings (inflexions) of some kind which are added to the stems of verbs to show person, number, and tense. Modern English has fewer than most, retaining only a remnant of the much more complex system present in Old English.

Old English had the following inflexions in the present tense:

first person singular (I)	*-e*
second person singular (thou)	*-ast* or *-east*
third person singular (he, she, it)	*-ath* or *-eth*
plural (we, you, they)	*-ath* or *-en*

This system was already being gradually eroded before the Norman Conquest, when the interaction of Anglo-Saxons with the Danes, who spoke a very closely related language, helped to iron out the inflexions which made understanding difficult. In Middle English, the plural ending was *-eth* in the south, *-en* in the Midlands, and *-es* in the north, where the third person singular was also *-es*. By the 16th century the plural inflexions had fallen out of use, while the northern *-es* had been adopted in London English for the third person singular. Shakespeare used both *-eth* and *-es* for this (writing *she driveth* but *he dreames*, for example). The language of the King James Bible, and of 'traditional language' church services, follows a pattern which survived in use until the 17th century, using *-est* for the second person singular (**thou**) and *-eth* for the third person singular.

> I come, thou com*est*, he com*eth*, we come, you come, they come

The only inflexion to survive into modern English is the third person singular ending, which has now become *-s*, except after sounds like *s*, *z*, *ch*, and *sh*, where it is *-es*, with the vowel still pronounced (e.g. *tosses*, *buzzes*, *catches*, *pushes*).

Thou survived in Quaker use until at least the late 19th century, together with **thee**, used for the object of the sentence (like **him** instead of **he**), and the possessive forms **thy** and **thine**. These may still be heard in certain communities where traditional dialect is spoken, often in forms such as *tha* and *thi*. Some verbs had their own particular forms, such as *thou dost*, *he doth*, *thou art*.

Nouns also originally had inflexions, but the only regular ones to survive are the *-s* forming plurals and the *-'s* forming possessives.

No one, thank goodness, has ever asked, 'What is the difference between American and British English?' But we get many enquiries on aspects of American English and, if someone were to ask the big question, this is the sort of answer they might get.

This is a huge subject, and I can give you only a brief outline. American English differs from British English in hundreds of details, while maintaining a common grammar and vocabulary that allows the two nations to communicate. When discussing differences it should be remembered that American English has many dialects and variant forms, just as British English does, and that a Black New Yorker and a Californian might have as much difficulty understanding each other as a Devonshire farmer and a Glaswegian. The differences listed here are those between the standard varieties of British and American English.

Pronunciation:

The most noticeable characteristics are:

An **r** following a vowel (e.g. in **bear, turn**) is discernible in American English.

A **t** between vowels (e.g. in **tomato**) is pronounced as *d*.

Following **d, n, s,** and **t,** the sound you is pronounced *oo*, giving *noo* (new), *rezoom* (resume), *Toosday* (Tuesday), etc.

In words like **clerk** and **derby, er** is pronounced as in *herd*.

In words of four or more syllables with the main stress on the first or second, there is a strong secondary stress on the last syllable but one, and the vowel is fully enunciated, giving '**nec**ess-*airy*' (necessary), '**con**tem-*play*tive' (contemplative), etc.

Four vowels in British English, the *a* of **bat**, the *ah* of **dance** and **father**, the *o* of **hot**, and the *aw* of **law**, are represented by three vowels, *a*, *ah*, and *aw*, used somewhat differently: *a* in **bat, dance, fasten,** *ah* in **father, hot, conflict,** *aw* in **law, long**.

Words ending in *-ile* reduce the vowel in the last syllable, giving '*missle*' (missile), '*dossil*' (docile), '*fertle*' (fertile) and '*steral*' (sterile).

Many words are stressed differently, e.g. adver**tise**ment, **lab**oratory, de**tail**, re**search**.

Some words adopted from other languages are pronounced differently, e.g. '*dee-po*' (depot); '*thee-ayter*' is sometimes heard for theatre.

Spelling:

American spelling is often more straightforward and regular than British, partly as a result of reforms suggested by the great lexicographer Noah Webster (1758–1843), who in 1828 produced the first truly American dictionary. He introduced *-or* in preference to *-our* (color, favor), *-er* rather than *-re* (theater, center), *e* for *oe* (see p. 89) and *ae* (anesthetic, hemorrhage), *-se* for *-ce* (defense, pretense; for **licence** and **practice** see p. 52) and such simplifications as *ax*, *program*, *check* (cheque), *plow*, *mold*. Some of his other suggestions, such as *bred*, *frend*, *helth*, *beleeve*, *yeer*, *rong*, *ritten*, *tung*, *munth*, *korus*, *mashine*, *bilt*, *obleek*, *laf* (laugh) and *examin* (examine) did not catch on—it would have been interesting to see the results if they had.

In words which may be spelt *-ise* or *-ize* in British English, *-ize* is always used in American English (see p. 59).

Words such as **backward(s)**, **eastward(s)**, **toward(s)** do not have an *s* in American English.

Some verbs which in British English double the final consonant when a suffix is added often do not do so in American English, e.g. **traveled**, **traveler**, **kidnaped**, **worshiped**, **combated**.

Vocabulary:

Though Webster advocated change, he produced his dictionary in response to changes that had already happened to the vocabulary of American English, which made British English dictionaries unsatisfactory. Words such as **congress**, **senator**, and **marshal** were being used in new ways to describe new systems, and American words were being coined for American things, such as **prairie**, **mustang**, **gopher**, and **hominy**.

British English was already rich with words from the languages of neighbours, trading partners, and colonies. To this word-hoard the Americans added words from the Native American tribes, from European colonists of the New World, and from later immigrants. While some of these words remain distinctly American, many are now world English.

From Spanish came **barbecue, plaza, stampede, enchilada, sombrero, alligator, marijuana,** and **stevedore,** from French **bayou, butte, crevasse, levee, chowder,** and **gopher** (from *gaufre* 'honeycomb', because of the creatures' burrows 'honeycombing' the ground), from Dutch **waffle, coleslaw, cookie, caboose, sleigh, boss, snoop,** and **spook**. Native Americans furnished **chinook, caucus, skunk,** and **mackinaw,** as well as words such as **tomahawk, kayak, igloo, moccasin,** and **tepee** which referred to their lifestyle, and **caribou, toboggan,** and **chocolate** which came in via French. From Africa came **jigger** (a tropical flea), **okra, yam,** and **zombie**; the famous saying *speak softly and carry a big stick, and you will go far*, commonly attributed to Theodore Roosevelt, may be of West African origin. German immigrants brought **nix, spiel, loafer, semester, pumpernickel, dunk,** and **hamburger** (see p. 154); **brainwash** and **gung-ho** are from Chinese, **honcho** from Japanese, and Yiddish-speaking immigrants donated **chutzpah, kibitzer, schlemiel,** and **schmuck**.

As well as coining new words, the Americans also kept some words, and forms such as **gotten** (see p. 83), which became obsolete in British English. They still use **turnpike** for a road which one has to pay to use (a toll-free highway is a **freeway**). Despite opposition to such 'Americanisms', some have come back into British English: **guess** for 'suppose' was used by Chaucer and **mad** for 'angry' by Shakespeare.

Many everyday words are different in American English:

British English	*American English*
adrenalin	epinephrine
bath	tub
biscuit	cookie

British English	*American English*
bring up (children)	raise
curtains	drapes
deck chair	beach chair
draughts (the game)	checkers
dressing gown	bathrobe *or* robe
dustbin	trashcan *or* garbage can
lift	elevator
patience (the game)	solitaire
pavement	sidewalk
petrol	gasoline *or* gas
rise (in pay)	raise *or* increase
rubbish *or* refuse	garbage
terrace house	row house

Sometimes the same word has a slightly different form:

British English	*American English*
aeroplane	airplane
aluminium	aluminum
baby's bottle	baby bottle
crayfish	crawfish
doll's house	dollhouse
maths	math
railway	railroad
sanatorium	sanitarium
windscreen	windshield

Familiar words may have different meanings in American English:

jelly (as also in Scots English) often refers to what the English would call **jam**; Americans sometimes use the trade name **jello** to denote the dessert.

corn denotes what the British call **maize.**

a **davenport** in British English is an ornamental desk with drawers and a sloped writing surface; an American davenport is a large, heavily upholstered sofa.

mean usually denotes 'nasty' rather than 'stingy' to Americans.

a **clever idea** or a **scheme** are both seen as devious, more like a 'cunning plan'.

biscuits are small scone-like balls of cooked dough, eaten with meat and gravy.

an American **vest** is a British **waistcoat**.

a **depot** can be a railway or bus station, or a bus garage.

theater often refers to a **cinema**; some Americans use the European spelling *theatre* to denote 'live theater'.

Colonial in British English refers to a colony; in American English it refers to the period before American Independence in 1776.

There are also some different constructions:

British English	*American English*
a quarter to five	a quarter of five
a quarter past five	a quarter after five
apart from	aside from
at school	in school
behind	back of *or* in back (of)
different from or to	different than
have got	have
have not got	do not have
I have just eaten	I just ate
in hospital	in the hospital
in the street	on the street
teach (i.e. be a teacher)	teach school
up to and including	through
(have a) wash, get washed	wash up
wash up, do the washing up	wash *or* do the dishes

As one might expect, there are also terms that Americans regard as quaintly British:

British English	*American English*
a bit, a spot of	a little
nearly	almost
ought	should
match	game

British English	*American English*
side	team
pitch	field
sport	sports
shut (of a shop etc.)	closed
packet (of cigarettes)	pack
properly	right *or* correctly
price rise	price increase
at the seaside	by the sea
be keen on	really like
coach	bus
fortnight	two *or* a couple of weeks
round	around
village	small town (except for Greenwich Village)
holiday	vacation (except for public holidays)
to some extent	some
very	real
certainly	sure

The relationship between British and American English is not static. Many words and phrases which started life across the Atlantic are now firmly naturalized in Britain, for example **to fall for, to fly off the handle, to snoop**. Some are familiar to many British people but still not part of ordinary usage, e.g. **feisty** (see p. 19), **tacky** meaning 'seedy, tatty, in poor taste'; and some have yet to work their passage (a personal favourite is **scofflaw**, a petty criminal or one who habitually flouts laws which are difficult to enforce, for example by parking illegally and not paying the fines).

It has been suggested that the languages will continue to diverge until the two nations will no longer be able to understand one another. Perhaps Noah Webster envisaged this; in their new and hard-won independence perhaps Americans would have welcomed the thought. But with the ease of global communications and the constant exchange of popular music, films, and television, the prospect looks less likely today than it did, say, fifty years ago.

In our dictionaries we include American vocabulary (suitably labelled) and we also give American spelling variants. We do not give American pronunciations, although some dictionaries intended for learners do. Both British and American English are taught all over the world, and learners' dictionaries therefore give more attention to the two varieties than those for native speakers; a browse through an advanced learners' dictionary will reveal many more differences than I have been able to list here.

Standard English is full of traps for the unwary; especially those words which look as though they ought to mean the same thing. The difficulties they cause are indicated by our post-bag, and by the fact that whole dictionaries of 'confusables' have been published. Here are some of the most commonly queried, listed alphabetically by the first word:

Q ABUSE/MISUSE

As nouns, both mean 'wrong or improper use'. However, **abuse** is the stronger of the two and often has moral overtones. As a verb, abuse tends to mean to use wrongly or badly (e.g. *to abuse one's authority*) or to treat badly (e.g. *to physically abuse a child*); it can also mean to malign or insult. **Misuse** means to use for an unsuitable purpose, or for a purpose not intended, e.g. misusing public funds by spending them on useless projects or for private gain, or misusing a knife by putting food into one's mouth with it or trying to use it as a screwdriver.

Q AFFECT/EFFECT

To **affect** something is to change or influence it in some way. However, to **effect** something is to make it happen; this word is rather more formal in tone. Confusingly, either 'affecting' something or 'effecting' something may bring about an **effect** or result.

The stability of the wall was affected by passing lorries.

The lorries had an adverse effect on the stability of the wall.

The demolition of the wall was effected by the detonation of a charge of dynamite.

The dynamite had a dramatic effect on the appearance of the wall.

Note that the dynamite did not merely 'affect' (influence) the demolition of the wall: it actually caused it.

Q ASSUME/PRESUME

Both can mean 'suppose'. **Presume** is used particularly when the supposition is based on evidence: *I presume she's gone, her coat's not here.* **Assume** takes something for granted without proof: *I assume she's gone* (I don't know that she has, but I've no reason to think otherwise). It can also mean to accept something temporarily for the sake of argument: *Assuming she's gone, do you want to leave a message?*

Q ASSURANCE/INSURANCE

In the insurance industry, **assurance** is for something that is *certain* to happen, **insurance** for something that *may* happen. You take out life assurance so that money is paid to your family *when* you die, and car insurance so that you are compensated *if* your car is wrecked or stolen.

Q ASSURE/ENSURE/INSURE

Assure and **ensure** both mean 'to guarantee'. The difference is between passive and active; if success is assured, it will surely come; if you assure someone of something you tell them that it is definitely true and put their minds at rest; in neither case is any positive effort involved. If success is ensured, it will come because action has been taken to make sure that it does.

To **insure** something is to take out insurance to compensate for its loss or damage. *Insure* is also an alternative American spelling for *ensure*.

Q DELUSION/ILLUSION

A **delusion** is a false or misguided belief not based on evidence and impervious to argument, e.g. *he suffers from the delusion that he is Napoleon.* An **illusion** is a false impression based on the evidence of the senses, e.g. *the mirrors give an illusion of spaciousness*, or a false supposition, e.g. *poverty dispelled all her romantic illusions about life.* Someone witnessing or having an illusion may know or find out that it is not true; they may even enjoy it. A delusion, on the other hand, is a serious matter and very hard to shift.

Q DISINTERESTED/UNINTERESTED

Disinterested means impartial, having nothing to gain or lose by the outcome. **Uninterested** means apathetic, finding no interest in something. As an example, an uninterested observer of a horse-race finds the whole thing tedious; another observer may enjoy the spectacle but be disinterested because he or she has not placed a bet.

Disinterested seems to be used more and more often to mean 'apathetic' (which incidentally was its original meaning). It may be better to use **impartial** if there is a danger of being misunderstood, although this does not include the idea of having nothing to gain or lose.

Q DISSATISFIED/UNSATISFIED

Unsatisfied means unhappy because you lack, or have too little of, whatever it is you desire. **Dissatisfied** means unhappy or angry because what you have is not what you want. Both can refer to material or immaterial things.

The meanings overlap to a certain extent, in that being unsatisfied or unfulfilled may cause dissatisfaction. For example, you may end a meal unsatisfied (still hungry), and this might make you feel dissatisfied (irritable). However, if you ate your fill but the food was of poor quality, you would not be unsatisfied (because you had had enough) but you would probably be dissatisfied because you did not enjoy it.

Q ENQUIRY/INQUIRY

Inquiry tends to be more formal than **enquiry,** and is often used for an official investigation, e.g. *a public inquiry* or *a police inquiry*. **Enquiry** is used for a less formal question, e.g. *an enquiry to OWLS*. **Inquire** and **enquire** are used in a similar way; inquire meaning to undertake a formal or official investigation, enquire meaning simply to ask a question.

Q FEWER/LESS

The difference is that **less** means 'not as much', whereas **fewer** means 'not as many': *a shower uses less water than a bath, so take fewer baths and more showers*. This is sometimes tricky when referring to quantities. In *less than six weeks* **less** is used because 'six weeks' does not mean six separate weeks but a single period of time lasting six weeks. Similarly, in *he had less than £30*, £30 is a single sum of money; *he had fewer than 30 pounds* would imply that he did not have as many as 30 pound coins.

Q HISTORIC/HISTORICAL

Historic means 'important in history' and refers to something in the past that changed the course of events or something in the present that will be regarded as important in times to come: *a historic battle*; *the historic treaty of Maastricht*. **Historical** refers to something that actually existed in the past (*was King Arthur a historical figure, or just a legend?*), to a literary work that deals with the past (*a historical novel*), or to something belonging to the past with no implications for the present (*a practice long abandoned, of purely historical interest*). It also means 'because of past events': *for historical reasons the Montagues and Capulets don't mix*.

Q HYPOTHESIS/THEORY

A **hypothesis** is a possible explanation put forward to account for a set of facts or phenomena, intended as a basis for discussion or trial. A hypothesis is a tool to think with: there is no assumption that it is true. A **theory** is an explanation based on general principles which, although not proved, seems to account for all the facts and is generally accepted as true.

Q INOCULATION/VACCINATION

Strictly speaking, **vaccination** applies only to the practice of protecting someone against smallpox by introducing cowpox virus into the body (vaccinate comes ultimately from Latin *vacca* 'cow'). **Inoculation** refers to protection against any disease by introducing a small amount of the disease-causing organism in order to stimulate the body's immune response. However the preparations used are called **vaccines** so one could be said to be vaccinated against many diseases. 'Inoculation' is the preferred form in medical circles and is becoming more popular outside; 'vaccination' is still used but is beginning to sound old-fashioned.

Q MONOLOGUE/SOLILOQUY

A **monologue** is a dramatic sketch performed by one actor; it has a narrative structure and may have several characters which the actor may imitate without attempting to act the role fully. The actor will normally show awareness of the audience and tell the story to them. Monologue is also applied to a long and usually boring speech that monopolizes a conversation. A **soliloquy** is an expression of one's private thoughts. An actor performing a soliloquy will not show awareness of the audience; as far as they are concerned he is alone and thinking aloud.

Q OPHTHALMOLOGIST/OPTICIAN

An **ophthalmologist** is a physician who specializes in diseases and defects of the eye. An **optician** makes and sells all kinds of lenses and optical devices, but the term **ophthalmic optician** is used for a person qualified to test the eyesight and prescribe lenses, and **dispensing optician** for one who supplies spectacles.

Q OPOSSUM/POSSUM

These are both marsupials. **Opossums** are members of the family Didelphidae, native to America. **Possums** belong to the family Phalangeridae, native to Australia and New Zealand. Confusion arises because the American animal is also called **possum** in colloquial speech; you have to know where the animal comes from.

Q ORIENT/ORIENTATE

The two words are virtually synonymous. **Orientate** is currently preferred in general use in Britain. **Orient** predominates in technical use and in the USA, which seems to be encouraging its use in Britain. In time it may be the preferred form; for the moment it is a matter of personal choice.

Q PARTIALLY/PARTLY

These mean almost the same and are often used interchangeably. **Partially** means 'not completely or fully'; a partially sighted person has limited sight. **Partly** means 'in part, not wholly' and is usually used of material things: *it's partly metal and partly plastic*. The slight difference in meaning is best shown by an example: something that is partially cooked is underdone; if it is partly cooked then some of it is cooked (perhaps even burned), while other parts are not.

Q PRINCIPAL/PRINCIPLE

Principal can be a noun or an adjective. As an adjective it means 'main, chief, most important': *coal was a principal export*; *the campaign's principal objective*. As a noun it denotes an important person, e.g. the head of a college or a leading performer in a play, concert, or opera, or the actual perpetrator of an action, particularly as opposed to an agent or representative. It also refers to a sum invested, as opposed to the income from it. **Principle** exists only as a noun, meaning a general scientific law (*the principles of physics*) or a fundamental belief or moral rule guiding one's actions (*we must not abandon our principles*).

Q SHALL/WILL

Both are used to express a future action or intention; strictly speaking, **shall** should be used in the first person and **will** in the second or third, although will is now often used for all, especially in speech, and is usual in American English. If the normal order is reversed it implies determination: *I shall drown and no one will save me* is a plaintive statement of fact, *I will drown and no one shall save me* expresses a pigheaded insistence on drowning despite everyone's best efforts. This reversal can also be used to express a promise or vow: *I won't tell a soul*; *they shall not pass*; *you shall go to the ball.*

Q TAX AVOIDANCE/TAX EVASION

Very important to know the difference between these! **Tax avoidance** is the legitimate activity of avoiding liability for tax, e.g. by claiming all one's allowances, investing money in ways which attract tax concessions, or by making gifts to one's heirs to avoid inheritance tax. **Tax evasion** is failing to pay tax for which one is liable, e.g. by not declaring all one's income, claiming allowances one is not entitled to, or simply not responding to the demand for payment.

Q WHO'S/WHOSE

Who's is an abbreviated form of 'who has' or 'who is': *who's broken the window?*; *who's going to pay for it?* **Whose** is a relative pronoun meaning 'of whom' or 'of which': *the person whose ball broke it should pay*; *the house whose window was broken.* It also means 'of whom' (but not 'of which') in questions: *whose ball was it, anyway?*

Sometimes a change in spelling can make all the difference:

Q DEPENDANT/DEPENDENT

In British English, **dependant** is the noun (*children and other dependants*); **dependent** is the adjective (*dependent relatives*;

heavily dependent on oil imports). In American English the adjective is the same but the noun may be spelt either way.

Q HANGED/HUNG

Hung is the usual form of the past tense and past participle of 'to hang'. **Hanged** is used only for the sense of 'to hang by the neck until dead'. An artist's pictures might be hung in the Royal Academy; if he were hanged there, the police would be called to investigate.

Q LICENCE/LICENSE

In British English the noun is **licence** (*driving licence, poetic licence*), **license** is the verb (*licensed to sell alcohol*). Premises on which alcohol may be sold may be **licensed** (having obtained official permission) or **licenced** (possessing a licence). In American English both are usually spelt **license**.

Q PRACTICE/PRACTISE

In British English **practice** is the noun (*piano practice, a doctor's practice, our usual practice*); **practise** is the verb (*practise the piano, practise as a solicitor, practise what you preach*). In American English either spelling may be used for the noun or the verb, but both are usually spelt **practice**.

We are asked not only about different words, but different things:

Q What's the difference between a STOAT and a WEASEL? Which one is an ermine?

According to the old joke, a weasel's so 'weaselly' recognized because a stoat's 'stoatally' different! In fact they are quite similar; the main difference is in the size, which can be difficult to judge. The **stoat** (*Mustela erminea*) is larger (12–18 inches 30–45 cm) and has a longish tail with a black tip. The **weasel** (*Mustela nivalis*) is smaller (25 cm) and has no black tip to its tail. You are more likely to see a weasel than a stoat; the stoat avoids human habitation and is mainly nocturnal, whereas the weasel will live in country or town and may be active at any time. The stoat is called ermine especially when it has turned white in winter; the dark marks in ornamental ermine fur are the tips of the tails, which stay black.

Q I went to buy some SUPERGLUE, but was told the shop didn't stock it. They sold me some 'contact adhesive', which seems to me to be the same thing. Were they being funny?

No, they were being precise. Although it is often used for any kind of strong glue which sticks immediately, **Superglue** is a trade name.

Q Is there any difference between a PUB and an INN?

Not in modern use. In the past an **inn** was obliged to provide food and accommodation for travellers, whereas a **public house** only served drinks and was used mainly by the locals. Nowadays, with more and more pubs serving food and perhaps having one or two rooms for the bed and breakfast trade, the difference has disappeared. Any pub can call itself an inn, and punning names such as the *Welcome Inn* or *Dewdrop Inn* can be seen on small premises with no kitchen or rooms for an overnight stay.

Q Are SILICON and SILICONE different things, or just different spellings for the same thing?

Silicon is a non-metallic element, abundant in the earth's crust but not occurring naturally except in combination. Silicon dioxide (silica) occurs as quartz and as the main constituent of many other rocks. Pure silicon is widely used in electronics because of its conductive properties, and is the substance found in *silicon chips*, minute semi-conductors carrying electric circuits.

Silicone refers to any of the various compounds of silicon and oxygen which are used as waterproofing or insulating agents, and in polishes, lubricants, and what are delicately described as 'cosmetic implants'.

Q STALACTITES and STALAGMITES—which is which?

A **stalactite** grows down from a cave roof, a **stalagmite** grows up from the floor. I was taught to remember the difference by thinking of ants in the pants: the 'mites' go up and the 'tights' come down. Another memory-jogger is that staIaCtites grow from the Ceiling (and must hold on 'tight'), while stalaGmites grow from the Ground (and 'might' eventually reach the ceiling).

Q What's the difference between *Art Nouveau* and *Art Deco*?

Art Nouveau is a style of art, architecture, and decoration which developed in the late 19th century from the romanticism of the Pre-Raphaelites. It is characterized by curving, organic lines, intertwining vines of flowers and leaves, and the use where possible of natural materials. It is associated in Britain with Aubrey Beardsley and William Morris; Guimard's designs for the Paris Métro are also famous.

Art Deco is applied mainly to a style of decorative art and interior design in the 1920s and 1930s, although it is sometimes extended to similar styles in architecture and painting. It takes its name from the *Exposition Internationale des Arts Décoratifs et Industriels*, held in Paris in 1925. It is characterized by geometric patterning, clean, simple lines, classical Greek and Egyptian motifs, and the use of modern materials such as stainless steel and Bakelite as well as enamel, bronze, and polished stone. Art Deco is also sometimes called *art moderne*, causing confusion with the older Art Nouveau.

Q I've been watching the ice-skating on the telly all

week and I still can't tell the difference between the jumps. Can you enlighten me?

All the jumps involve a rotation in the air; a double jump involves two turns, a triple three, and so on.

An **axel** is a jump with one-and-a-half turns, taking off from the front outside edge of one skate and landing on the back outside edge of the other.

A skater performing a **lutz** takes off from the back outside edge of one skate and lands on the back outside edge of the other; for a **salchow** he takes off from the back inside edge of one skate and lands on the back outside edge of the other.

A **loop jump** involves taking off and landing on the back outside edge of the same foot; in a **toe loop (jump)** the take-off is assisted by the toe of the other foot.

Since investigating these terms I have also been watching the skating and find that, although in theory I now know what they are, I still have to wait for the commentator to tell me what I've just seen.

Q I'm a bit confused by the terms 'vintage', 'veteran', and 'classic' applied to cars. The first two I believe are something to do with age, but what about classic?

The distinction is not clear cut. The Veteran Car Club of Great Britain classes cars built before 1917 as **veterans** and those built before 1905 as **true veterans. Vintage** cars are those built between 1917 and 1930. Others take **vintage** cars as those made between 1905 and 1930, a **veteran** being older. Vintage cars have also been called **classic** cars, but in recent years **classic** has come to be used of a car of such good design and quality that it is still desirable long after other cars of its age have been scrapped. A classic car can be of any age; I have even seen a modern sports car referred to as 'the classic of the future'.

And finally, one that's been puzzling scholars ever since Hamlet claimed to know the difference:

Q How *do* you know a hawk from a handsaw?

That depends on what you mean by **hawk** and what you mean by **handsaw**.

There are several possible meanings of **hawk**: the bird of prey and a clearing of the throat are both recorded early enough to have been known to Shakespeare. **Hawk** was a 19th-century dialect word for a dung fork: far too late for Shakespeare, but believed to be a variant of **hack**, applied to various agricultural implements including those for chopping and cutting, and recorded from the 14th century. As a word for a grating in a river to catch fish, **hawk** is not recorded until the mid-17th century, but **heck**, with the same meaning, is earlier. The first citation in *OED* for **hawk** as a plasterer's tool is dated 1700; later research incorporated into the *New Shorter Oxford English Dictionary* has established a late Middle English date.

A **handsaw** was a saw used with one hand (as opposed to the large saws worked by two men); Shakespeare uses it in this sense in *Henry IV Part 1*. However, this struck scholars as so far removed from any of the 'hawks' that they have from time to time suggested alternatives, the most popular being **heronshaw** or **hernshaw** (a heron, particularly a young one) and **handsel** (a gift). Herons were hunted with hawks, and it was no doubt a good thing to be able to tell your own bird from a young heron. It has been suggested that **hawk** might mean 'an instance or an attempt at selling' (related to the verb hawk) and that (if the other word were handsel) Hamlet was able to tell the difference between being sold something and being given it, or between a gift and something with strings attached—unfortunately, **hawk** is not recorded in this sense.

It should be fairly easy to tell a hawk from a handsaw, although the exact difference will depend on what each is.

Perhaps a hawk is a bird and a handsaw is just that, and Shakespeare picked two things not in the least like each other to puzzle Hamlet's listeners—and us.

4

What is the correct way of . . .?

One of the greatest difficulties in writing dictionaries for ordinary use is the balancing of two different aims: describing actual usage accurately ('descriptive lexicography'), and distinguishing between correct and incorrect usage ('prescriptive lexicography'). In fact, 'correct' usage is not graven in tablets of stone, but is simply the usage which is generally accepted among English speakers. What was perfectly acceptable to one generation may appear quite wrong to the next, and what is quite acceptable in ordinary conversation may not be appropriate in a formal speech or a business letter. The constant changing of the language affects it in all its aspects: pronunciation, spelling, grammar, punctuation, and word meanings and usage.

***Spelling** is a particularly important area of concern for many users of English, since an inability to spell is often taken to be a mark of poor education. The invention of printing did more than anything else to establish a standard for English spelling, but many people are unaware of the extent to which English is still* *very tolerant of certain variations. Though editors and others responsible for printed text have to prefer one form over another in the interests of consistency, it is not incorrect to use an accepted variant spelling.*

Trends and fashions in certain aspects of spelling (such as hyphenation) are changing very rapidly in current English, and it is impossible to revise every dictionary at once, so different dictionaries may show minor inconsistencies with each other as new editions come out at intervals.

The following letters illustrate some of the most common enquiries about spelling:

Q I have always spelt such verbs as 'privatize', 'standardize', etc. with *-ize* on the end, and my Oxford dictionary gives spellings ending in *-ize*, but my supervisor claims that this is an Americanism. Is it?

For a large number of words, both *-ize* and *-ise* spellings are quite acceptable in British English. It is true that the *-ize* spellings are standard in American English, but that does not mean that their use is simply an Americanism. The *-ize* form has always been an accepted alternative spelling in British use, and was for a long time generally preferred.

The suffix *-ize* comes ultimately from the Greek verb stem *-izein*. In both English and French, many words with this ending have been adopted (usually via Latin), and many more have been invented by adding the suffix to existing words. In modern French the verb stem has become *-iser*, and this may have encouraged the use of *-ise* in English, especially as some of these verbs have come to us via French (e.g. *civilize*, from French *civiliser*). It is slightly paradoxical that many British English speakers now regard *-ize* as an Americanism; if anything, the Americans have avoided the influence of French, and *-ise* could be regarded as a Gallicism.

Nevertheless, American usage has introduced *-z-* into some words in which it was not originally regarded as standard, and some of these spellings have become standard American

usage. There are two main groups of words in which *-ise* is always used in British English, including some very common ones. (If you always use *-ise* then it does at least save you from having to remember these exceptions.) The groups are:
1. Words in which the ending is not pronounced 'eyes', such as *expertise*, *precise*, and *promise*.
2. Verbs that correspond to nouns ending in *-ise*, or have *-is-* as part of the stem of the word (e.g. *advertisement*, from French *avertissement*, so *advertise*). Many of these are from the Latin stems *-cis-* (e.g. *incise*), *-vis-* (e.g. *televise*: compare *television*), or *-mis-* (e.g. *surmise*).

The *Oxford Guide to English Usage* has a list of the more common ones:

advertise	*enterprise*
advise	*excise*
apprise	*exercise*
arise	*improvise*
chastise	*incise*
circumcise	*merchandise*
comprise	*premise*
compromise	*prise* (*open*)
demise	*revise*
despise	*supervise*
devise	*surmise*
disguise	*surprise*
enfranchise	*televise*

Whatever the reason, the *-ise* spelling has become very common in British use, and it is up to you which form you use, provided that you are consistent within a single piece of writing (and follow any required company 'house style'). Oxford dictionaries published in the United Kingdom generally show both forms where they are in use, but give *-ize* first as it reflects both the origin and the pronunciation more closely, while indicating that *-ise* is an allowable variant. Some dictionaries, such as the *Australian Concise Oxford Dictionary*, now give *-ise* as the first form, with *-ize* as the alternative.

Words for which *-ize* is acceptable in American but not British use include *apprize*, *comprize*, *merchandize*, and *prize* (*open*); American spelling also allows the highly irregular forms *analyze* and *paralyze*. Words which always end in *-ize* even in British use include *assize*, *baize*, *capsize*, *maize*, *seize*, and all words derived from *prize* (= 'to value') and *size*.

Q My dictionary has an entry for 'rain forest' as two words, but all the leaflets from a local conservation group spell it as one word, 'rainforest'. Which is correct?

Both are correct. Most dictionaries do not have space to give all the acceptable alternatives for compounds like this, and the choice is usually a matter of personal preference (or of conformity to house style). In fact, like many such words, this one has shifted in recent use, and such shifts gradually filter into the dictionaries. Very sharp-eyed readers of dictionaries will notice that while the eighth edition of the *Concise Oxford Dictionary* (1990) has **rain forest,** the eighth edition of the *Pocket Oxford Dictionary* (1992) has **rainforest,** and so does the *New Shorter Oxford English Dictionary* (1993).

Q When is it correct to use a HYPHEN in a word?

The use of the hyphen is a particularly variable and unpredictable feature of English spelling. The editors of the first *Concise Oxford Dictionary* wrote that 'after trying hard at an early stage to arrive at some principle that should teach us when to separate, when to hyphen, and when to unite the parts of compound words, we had to abandon the attempt as hopeless, and welter in the prevailing chaos'.

However, certain trends in modern use are clear. Most modern writers tend to use the hyphen much more rarely, and write many compounds as single words, especially where the two components are single syllables. Words such as *birdsong*, *eardrum*, *figurehead*, *lawbreaker*, *playgroup*, and *scriptwriter* are now more common without a hyphen. In the introduction to the eighth edition of the *Concise Oxford Dictionary*, the editor remarked, 'This is a welcome tendency, because the hitherto much overused hyphen can now enjoy an enhanced role as a syntactic link to avoid ambiguity.' In other words, the hyphen is most useful in linking two words which are used together with a particular meaning, as in *cost-benefit analysis*, and in making the distinction between confusing pairs:

twenty-odd people	*twenty odd people*
a third-world conflict	*a third world conflict*
a red crested bird	*a red-crested bird*

In certain contexts several hyphens may be used: *two-hundred-year-old trees* means 'trees aged two hundred', but *two hundred-year-old* trees means 'two trees aged one hundred', and *two hundred year-old trees* means '200 seedlings planted last year'.

The hyphen also functions in distinguishing word pairs such as *reform* and *re-form* (form again), and may distinguish noun and verb uses: *Rubber-stamp each page with a rubber stamp*. It usefully separates suffixes where a solid word would be confusing, e.g. in words ending in *-like* where the first part has more than one syllable (*violin-like*, *saucer-like*) or ends in the letter *l* (*eel-like*, *bell-like*). It is usually taken to be unnecessary in *goalless* and *soulless*, and is rapidly falling out of use in words such as *coordinate* and *cooperate*.

I have recently noticed a slight tendency to reintroduce unnecessary hyphens, producing spellings such as *re-iterate* and *un-remarked*, though this may just result from the careless use of word-processors with hyphenation programs. In general the hyphen is abandoned as a word becomes familiar and widely accepted: we still write *inter-American*, but if the word becomes very familiar it will probably follow the pattern set by *transatlantic*.

Q It is usual in Canada to use British spellings such as 'honour' and 'colour' rather than the American equivalents 'honor' and 'color', but I am confused by 'honorary', which seems to be spelt without a *u* even in British dictionaries.

The *-our* ending is characteristic of words which entered English through Norman French, though some have been respelt to conform to the pattern of *-or* words taken directly from Latin. The result is much inconsistency, since we write *ardour*, *colour*, *labour*, but *pallor*, *terror*, *torpor*.

The occurrence of *-u-* in derivatives of words ending in *-our* is largely arbitrary: we use *colourist* but *coloration*, *honourable* but *honorary*. To some extent, the spelling is dependent on origin. If the derived word has its own source in Latin (such as *honorary* from Latin *honorarius*, and *coloration* from French *coloration* or late Latin *coloratio*), then the *-u-* is not normally introduced. Unfortunately this is not much help, since by the time you know a word's origin you have probably already discovered how to spell it, and some words run against even this rule of thumb.

The American practice of dropping the *-u-* from *-our* was one of the spelling reforms championed by Noah Webster (see p. 40).

Q How many 'e's are there in 'prescrib(e)able'?

The usual rule when adding *-able* to words ending in silent *e* is to drop the *e*. However, in British spelling, the *e* is kept in words ending in *-ceable* and *-geable*, where the *e* affects the sound of the preceding consonant, words ending in a consonant followed by *-leable* (e.g. *whistleable*), and words ending in *-ee* (e.g. *refereeable*). There are also a number of other words where the *e* is often kept in British use, usually for reasons of pronunciation:

blameable	*hireable*
dyeable	*likeable*
giveable (but *forgivable*)	*liveable*

nameable *sizeable*
rateable *tameable*
ropeable *unshakeable*
shareable

A fuller discussion of *-able*, and also *-ible*, may be found in the *Oxford Guide to English Usage*.

Q Why is the word 'perjorative' not in my Oxford dictionary?

Because it does not exist, at least in that form. The word you are thinking of is spelt **pejorative**, and means 'unpleasant, depreciatory, disparaging, or belittling'. It has no connection with **perjury**, and is derived from the Latin word *pejorare* meaning 'to make worse'.

The number of words which are commonly misspelt is so large that we could not possibly give them here, and must refer the reader to sources such as the ***Oxford Spelling Dictionary****. Just for the record, though, if you can't find 'miniscule' in your dictionary, try looking under the word 'minuscule'!*

Q How do you spell PAPADUM?

As with many words borrowed from languages written in non-Roman alphabets, there is no universally recognized way of rendering the Tamil word *pappaḍam* in English spelling. The complete *Oxford English Dictionary* records almost every imaginable variant:

papadam, papadom, papadum, papodam, papodum, popadam, poppadom, poppadum, poppodam, puppadum, puppodam, puppodum.

The edition of the *Little Oxford Dictionary* produced by our Indian branch some years ago used the spelling *papaddam*, and the *New Shorter Oxford English Dictionary* also allows for *popadom*. *Poppadam* is recommended in the recent *Pocket Oxford Dictionary*, with *poppadom* and *popadam* also listed. Take your pick!

Q My dictionary lists the word EXTROVERT, but surely this is an error, as psychologists always spell this word 'extravert'.

The word **extravert** was originally coined with this spelling in 1915, based on the Latin preposition *extra*, and most psychologists have indeed tended to retain this spelling. However, in ordinary use the alternative spelling **extrovert** soon became established, mainly by analogy with **introvert**, and probably also because *extra-* at the beginning of an English word tends to mean either 'very' or 'additionally' (as in *extra-special* and *extra-safe*) or 'outside, beyond the limits of' (as in *extracurricular*). In this case, as in many such instances, the dictionary records the usage which is actually dominant, rather than the one which might be considered historically or technically preferable.

Q My dictionary lists 'CASTOR SUGAR' but it says 'CASTER SUGAR' on the packet: which is right?

Both are right. Our first records for these spellings are 1855 for 'castor' and 1894 for 'caster'. The *-or* spelling used to be dominant, but the modern preference seems to be for the *-er* form, perhaps following the lead of sugar manufacturers.

Q Where should I break the word WHEREVER if it comes at the end of a line? Neither 'where-ver' nor 'wher-ever' looks right.

If you really must divide this word, then we would recommend *wher-ever*. The principle of word-division is not easy to summarize, but it is based on the syllable structure of the word. *Wherever* is formed by the combination of *where* and *ever*, but the missing *e* is notionally the silent one from the end of *where*, and *ever* should be kept in one piece when dividing the word. A handy guide to word-breaks is available in the *Oxford Spelling Dictionary*.

The formation of plurals often causes particular difficulty to our correspondents, especially when there is some doubt as to whether an apostrophe should be used:

Q Is the correct plural of PIZZA spelt 'pizzas' or 'pizza's'?

Definitely *pizzas*. The regular plural in English is formed simply with *-s* (or *-es* for words ending in *-s*, *-x*, *-z*, *-sh*, or soft *-ch*). You should not introduce an apostrophe just because the word happens to end in a vowel. The use of *-'s* with an apostrophe generally indicates the possessive, and so *pizza's* means 'of the pizza'. As a plural ending, *-'s* is usually reserved for certain specific types of word where confusion might otherwise result. These are:

(*a*) the plurals of single letters:

There are only three ***s's*** *in 'Christmases'.*

(but for the capital letter, *Ss* would be acceptable)

Mind your ***p's*** *and* ***q's***.

(*b*) the plurals of abbreviations:

Mrs Jones has two ***pg's*** *[paying guests] at the moment.*

The treasurer has received six cheques and two ***IOU's***.

(but *IOUs* is common and acceptable)

(*c*) the plurals of numerals:

The house was built in the ***1860's***.

(but *1860s* is preferable)

(*d*) as an alternative spelling of the plurals of a very few short words:

We went to several club ***do's*** *last year.*

(but *dos* is acceptable)

While out with his third wife he met both his ***ex's***.

(but *exes* is acceptable)

I've had four ***yes's*** *for black coffee.*
(but *yeses* is acceptable; the usual plural of no is *noes*)

Unfortunately, confusion is still widespread, with greengrocers' signs being a particularly rich source of superfluous apostrophes, though one can understand the urge to add them in the plurals of abbreviated forms such as *cauli*. An Oxford supermarket once caused much comment among students by hanging up a huge sign reading *Soup's*. Such a misspelling is truly worthy of the teacher's red pen!

Q Is MONIES the correct plural of 'money'?

The plural **monies** dates from the time (the 16th–17th centuries) when the singular could be spelt *money* or *monie*, of which it would be the regular plural form. It has remained in general use as an alternative spelling, especially in some formal business and legal contexts. However, there is no particular reason why it should be used instead of the regular plural **moneys**.

Q When travelling abroad I have often seen plural nouns such as 'fruits' and 'accommodations', where the collective forms 'fruit' and 'accommodation' would be usual in Britain. Now I have come across 'equipments' in a British magazine about aircraft. Does this mean that these plurals are catching on in British English?

Several varieties of English spoken outside the United Kingdom show a tendency to regularize some of the peculiarities of English grammar. While the standard construction would be 'kinds of fruit' or 'types of accommodation', in some areas it is quite normal practice to construct regularized plurals. This is particularly true in Indian English, where constructions such as *six aircrafts, they left their luggages at the station, he is a man of tastes*, etc. are quite common. Further examples are given in *Indian and British English* by

P. Nihalani and others. **Accommodations** for 'somewhere to stay' is quite common in the USA.

However, **equipments** has in fact been established in British use since the late 18th century, though it is now very unusual and is only seen in particular contexts such as formal military use.

Some people are puzzled or even offended by plurals of normally uncountable nouns such as *music* or *geometry*, but this represents a standard feature of English whereby an uncountable noun such as *geometry* may become countable if applied in extended senses such as 'a particular kind of geometry' (*The theorems of Euclid are sometimes contradicted in alternative geometries*) or 'the geometrical features of a particular thing' (*The varying geometries of snail shells*).

Q I am writing an article and have to refer to a number of 'children's games'. Have I put the apostrophe in the right place?

Yes. Plurals which do not end in the letter *-s* form the possessive case by the addition of *-'s*, so the correct form is *children's*. The ambiguity in a phrase such as 'several children's games' (the games of several different children, or several different games played by children?) is just unfortunate. The two senses can be distinguished by intonation when speaking, but not, of course, in writing.

Q I always thought that the correct plural of 'octopus' was 'octopi', but my dictionary gives only 'octopuses'.

The plurals of English words of Greek and Latin origin are rather variable, and the form of each one usually depends on how well established the word is. It may also depend on whether the original Latin or Greek plural is easy to recognize or pleasant to the English ear (which probably explains why *crocuses* is often preferred to *croci*).

The 'correct' plural of *octopus* would be *octopodes*, but this is rarely if ever seen, and *octopi* and *octopuses* are both widely used. Although *octopi* has been used for longer, it is not any more correct. In fact, it is an erroneous form, based on the mistaken idea that *octopus* is a Latin word of the second declension, whereas it is actually a Latinized form of the Greek word *oktōpous* (plural *oktōpodes*).

Other words ending in *-us* show a very unpredictable pattern. *Hippopotami*, like *octopi*, now tends to be regarded as pedantic or humorous, and *hippopotamuses* is usual. *Isthmi* is rare, and *omnibi* is usually a joke (and is quite ungrammatical from a Latin point of view). *Termini*, however, seems to be preferred in most instances, rather than the Anglicized form *terminuses*. *Syllabuses* is slightly more common than *syllabi*, but *cacti* is preferred to *cactuses* and *gladioli* to *gladioluses*. *Funguses* and *nucleuses* have scarcely ever been used at all.

Genus is from a different class of noun and the usual plural is the Greek form *genera*; the Latin plural of *magnum opus* is *magna opera*, but in English the easier *magnum opuses* tends to be adopted. *Plus* is not a noun in Latin, and the English plural is variable, with *pluses* marginally commoner than *plusses*.

Both *aquaria* and *aquariums* have been in use since the last century, and though scientists still tend to refer to 'aquaria', popular usage shows a slight preference for 'aquariums'. Perhaps it is significant that our files record the names of the American Association of Zoological Parks and *Aquariums*, but the European Community Association of Zoos and *Aquaria*. *Curricula* is usually preferred to *curriculums* (and should not be confused with the adjective, *curricular*). Usage is evenly balanced between *compendia* and *compendiums*, neither being very common.

Q Is DATA plural or singular?

Strictly speaking, **data** is the plural of **datum**, and should be used (like *facts*) with a plural verb. However, there has been a growing tendency to use it as an equivalent to *information*, followed by a singular verb, and this is now regarded as acceptable in American use and in the language of information technology. The traditional usage is still preferable, but to insist on it may appear pedantic, and could soon be a lost cause. **Data** may eventually go the way of **agenda**. This word was originally the plural of *agendum* 'thing to be done'. However, it became applied (as a singular) to the list of things to be done, and has now acquired the plural *agendas*.

Q How do you know when to put an apostrophe in *IT'S*?

The word *it's* is always short for 'it is' (as in *It's raining*), or, in informal use, for 'it has' (as in *It's got six legs*).

The word *its* (no apostrophe) means 'belonging to it'. It is one of the set of words used as possessive pronouns (*my, your, his, her, its, our, their*) and none of them have apostrophes. (*One's* is now written with an apostrophe, though originally it did not have one.)

The following example contains five *it* words with the apostrophes placed correctly:

> *Look at my dog! It's put its paws into its dish and it's treading on its dinner.*

***Grammar** has begun to intrude into the question of spelling here, and often proves a difficult stumbling-block even for fluent users of English. We are often asked to say what is correct, especially where usage is controversial.*

Q Is it acceptable to use 'they' and 'their' instead of 'he' or 'she' and 'his or her'? It seems grammatically incorrect.

This problem is the subject of much debate in books on the usage of the English language. There are no hard and fast rules, only a number of different attitudes and opinions. If possible, it is best to recast the sentence to avoid the problem altogether.

It seems clear that the use of *they/their* with reference to single persons of undetermined sex is not new, and was used in formal contexts by reputable authors long before the current phase of 'political correctness': *A person can't help their birth* (W. M. Thackeray, *Vanity Fair*, 1848). It is used quite naturally by children and adults alike, especially following words such as *anyone* and *no one* which are strictly singular but imply more than one person. However, it is frequently the subject of criticism by stylists and others who think that grammar ought to be strictly logical.

The use of the word *themselves* after a singular noun, as in one version of Shakespeare's *Lucrece* (*Every one to rest themselves betake*), is also often criticized, but it is long established. In fact, the 'singular' form *themself* does exist, though it is scarcely accepted in standard use at present. Originally (from about 1400 to 1550) it was the usual spelling of 'themselves', and it is occasionally revived by modern writers as a convenient sex-neutral singular form. Whether this usage will be accepted by the English-speaking community at large remains to be seen, but *themself* has been adopted for official documents by the Government of Ontario, Canada, and this may represent the trend of the future.

Q I often read 'the majority of people are', but if MAJORITY is a singular word, shouldn't it be 'the majority of people is'?

Although according to strict rules of grammar 'the majority of people is' might appear to be correct, in fact it is a well-established practice, in Britain at least, to use 'are'. While the 'majority' is singular, the 'people' are plural, and it is the people who are being talked about. The singular verb would be correct if the majority itself were the main topic of the sentence:

The majority of the members are in favour of this policy.

The majority in favour of the Government is smaller than it was last year.

Several other expressions are treated in this way, including *a lot of* and *a number of*, as if they were quantifying words like *more* or *most*.

A number of people are waiting for the bus.

rather than

A number of people is (?) waiting for the bus.

But note the use of a singular verb when 'number' is the real subject of the sentence:

The number of people waiting for the bus is growing.

A similar problem arises with more conventional collective nouns, such as *committee*, *couple*, *crowd*, *government*, and *team*, because such nouns are used to refer both to the whole group as an entity, and to the members of the group. One might well prefer a singular in the sentence

The committee has now come to a decision.

but could hardly use it in

The committee have now taken their seats.

In such cases the verb may be singular or plural depending on whether the collective entity or its individual members is being emphasized.

Smith & Co. has increased its share of the market.

Smith & Co. are a bunch of cowboys.

Leeds United is at the top of the league.

Leeds United are winning: they have just scored another goal.

I have invited my family to tea and they are coming on Sunday.

The last examples show how collective nouns may need to be interpreted as plurals in order to form natural idiomatic sentences; it would be rather odd to say:

Leeds United is winning: it has just scored another goal.

I have invited my family to tea and it is coming on Sunday.

Some collective nouns scarcely ever take a singular verb.

We bought six eggs, but a couple were bad (not *was bad*).

Words such as *half* and *quarter* may also cause problems: one correspondent found the following sentence in a newspaper article about poor standards of English (!):

A quarter of students is poor at punctuation.

This is an attempt to be 'correct' by giving a singular verb with the singular noun 'quarter'. However, 'students' is plural, and so should the verb be. (Quoted words or expressions are singular: apples *are* fruit, but 'apples' *is* plural.) Words for fractions may apply to parts of a single object or of things considered *en masse*, in which case they are singular, but they may also apply to portions of a group, in which case they behave as collective plurals:

Half of this apple is bad.

Half of these apples are bad.

Half of this basket of apples is bad.

Half of the apples in this basket are bad.

Half of these apples is enough for a gallon of cider.

The last one is a bit tricky: here, 'half of these apples' is being treated *en masse* as an amount, and is treated as a collective singular with a singular verb.

Some nouns can be treated as either singular or plural. For example:

The headquarters of the company is in London.

The headquarters of the company are in London.

Either of these sentences is correct. Note: not 'either of these sentences are correct'; *either*, *neither*, and *each* all take singular verbs, though *none* may take a plural verb.

Q Which is correct: 'I lay on the floor' or 'I laid on the floor'?

The word **lay** is a problem, since there are actually two common words spelt this way. One is the present tense of a verb whose basic meaning is 'place (something) in a more or less horizontal position', with the past tense **laid**. The other is the past tense of a verb whose present tense is **lie**, with the basic meaning '*be* in a more or less horizontal position'. This can be illustrated by the following sentences:

You must lay a rug on the floor and then lie on it.

He laid a rug on the floor and then lay on it.

I have already laid a rug on the floor and lain on it.

I laid on the floor is not a complete sentence, and prompts one to ask: 'But what did you lay on the floor? (An egg?!)' As used to be said in the nursery: *Hens lay*, *little girls lie* (which introduces yet another ambiguity in the word *lie*)!

The instruction *lay on a rug* can only correctly mean 'provide a rug' (as in 'lay on a meal for six'), unless it is being used with an understood object ('lay [it] on a rug') in the elliptical style typical of recipes (as in 'lay on a rack and stand in a cool place').

Q Which is correct: 'my friend and I' or 'my friend and me'?

It depends on the context. In colloquial speech, **me** is often used where standard grammar would require **I**. Occasionally one hears **I** incorrectly used for **me** by people who remember being corrected as children but do not understand the reason for the correction. The simple rule of thumb is to remember that 'I' and 'me' will behave exactly as they would if your friend was not mentioned.

[My friend and] ***I*** *went to the cinema.*

Aunt Jo paid for [my friend and] ***me****.*

The film was a favourite of [my friend's and] ***mine****.*

[She and] ***I*** *caught the bus back; it was too far for [her and]* ***me*** *to walk.*

I can only be the subject of the sentence, and the object of the sentence must be **me**. Try missing out the bracketed parts of these examples:

Me [and my sister] went to the village school.

The mayor sent an invitation to [my husband and] I.

The result is faintly ridiculous, and a sure indication that the wrong word has been used. By the way, there is no rule about who comes first in the sentence, I or the other person.

Only in a few contexts is there a definite acceptable variation in the use of *I* and *me* (and *he/him* etc.). The most common is in the use of comparatives with *than*. In ordinary use it would be acceptable to say *My husband is older than me*, but it would also be formally correct to say *My husband is older than I*. In the second case, the sentence has been abbreviated from the full form, *My husband is older than I am*, and so it is justifiable to use *I* in this context.

In informal use *me* is often used for emphasis where *I* would be strictly correct, and to say *It is I* instead of *It's me* to announce one's arrival sounds absurdly grand. However, one might say *That was me ringing the doorbell*, but in formal writing it would be better to put *It was I who was ringing the doorbell*. Again, there is a quick test of formal correctness: who was ringing the doorbell? ***I*** *was ringing the doorbell* (not ***Me*** *was ringing the doorbell*).

Q My mother always told me off for saying OFF OF, but I've found that Samuel Pepys uses it in his diary. Is it acceptable after all?

Despite being used by several respectable authors, including Samuel Pepys (*These people . . . will run themselves off of their legs*, from the *Diary* for 25 Nov. 1668) and Samuel Richardson (*Got off of that, as fast as possible*, from *Clarissa*, ch. 5), this idiom is now regarded as non-standard, and is found only in informal or colloquial speech (especially in the USA), or in local dialects. *Off of* was commonly used in the 17th and 18th centuries where we might now use *away from*, *off from*, or *off* alone, especially in referring to a ship as being 'off of' a place on the coast. John Bunyan uses it in a similar way (*About a furlong off of the Porters Lodge*, from *Pilgrim's Progress*, ch. 1).

Shakespeare used 'off of' in *Henry VI Part* II, but only in the mouth of a dishonest peasant (*Suffolk: 'How cam'st thou so?' Simpcox: 'A fall off of a tree.'*), and by the time Mark Twain used it in *Huckleberry Finn* it was probably a mark of dialect or uneducated speech (*I'd borrow two or three dollars off of the judge for him*).

Q What are SPLIT INFINITIVES, and why should I avoid them?

Probably the most famous split infinitive is the one in the introduction to each episode of the vintage TV series *Star Trek*: *To boldly go where no man has gone before!* The infinitive is *to go*, and it is here split by the adverb *boldly*. Any such case where a word (usually an adverb) is inserted between *to* and its verb is a split infinitive: e.g. 'to slowly pour a drink', 'to narrowly miss the target', etc.

There is a widespread myth that split infinitives are bad grammar; indeed, it seems to be the only supposed 'rule of grammar' that many people know! Split infinitives were at one time a matter of serious controversy among teachers and grammarians. (Perhaps the 'rule' was influenced by the fact that Latin, whose grammar was drummed into all medieval students, has infinitives which consist of a single word and are therefore unsplittable.) However, they are not, strictly speaking, grammatically incorrect. They are in many contexts justifiably regarded as bad style, and are avoided on that account, but a well-constructed sentence may nevertheless contain one. Kazuo Ishiguro's prize-winning novel *The Remains of the Day* ends with a good example:

> *I should hope, then, that by the time of my employer's return, I shall be in a position to pleasantly surprise him.*

In the *Star Trek* example, to avoid the split infinitive would require 'to go boldly' or 'boldly to go': the first is weak and loses the rhythmic force of the original, and the second is over-formal and destroys a fine rhetorical sequence of phrases beginning with 'to', so there is a good case for retaining the split infinitive. In some sentences there may be no way of unsplitting the infinitive without changing the meaning of the sentence or at least making it ambiguous:

> *The committee decided to more than double the drinks budget.* (i.e. they decided to increase the drinks budget by more than 100 per cent)
>
> *The committee decided more than to double the drinks budget.* (i.e. they also decided something else as well as doubling the budget)
>
> *The committee decided to double more than the drinks budget.* (i.e. they decided to double something else too)

Fanatical split-infinitive-haters must rewrite such sentences altogether.

We recommend you to consciously stop worrying about split infinitives. If we said, 'We recommend you consciously to stop worrying about split infinitives', it could be the *recommending* that was conscious instead of the *stopping*. If we said, 'We recommend you to stop consciously worrying about split infinitives', we could be suggesting that you should stop worrying *consciously* but may continue to worry *unconsciously*.

The avoidance of unnecessary split infinitives is often good practice, preventing inelegant or awkward constructions: the sentence in the last paragraph might well begin, 'We recommend that you consciously stop . . .' However, far worse sentences are often created by the clumsy avoidance of split infinitives than by leaving them alone. The main problem with using a split infinitive is that some people, on hearing you use one, will blanch or wince, or impolitely correct you.

***Usage** in more general contexts is a frequent source of dispute, and we are often called upon to pronounce definitively, sometimes on questions where no definitive answer truly exists, though many of our correspondents know the answer they would like to hear!*

Q Can anything be done to stop people using BILLION in the American sense of 'a thousand million'? The British billion of 'a million million' seems much more logical, and there is a word 'milliard' for 'a thousand million'.

The 'American' billion is undoubtedly here to stay, and the French term *milliard* for 'a thousand million' has never achieved any real currency in English. Once businessmen and journalists found themselves discussing 'thousand millions' so frequently the American system simply became more convenient, despite any lack of logical tidiness; and it makes profits and budgets sound more impressive! It is now the standard usage in British government publications, and is rapidly establishing itself as the norm in other European languages too.

One minor advantage in the American system is the ease of expression of larger numbers without repeating 'thousand' all the time. The higher numbers work like this:

	American	*British*
10^{12}	trillion	billion
10^{15}	quadrillion	thousand billion
10^{18}	quintillion	trillion
10^{21}	sextillion	thousand trillion
10^{24}	septillion	quadrillion
10^{27}	octillion	thousand quadrillion
10^{30}	nonillion	quintillion
10^{33}	decillion	thousand quintillion

Q A pumpkin is defined as a FRUIT, but my *Concise Oxford Dictionary*, which is the sixth edition, also lists it in the entry for VEGETABLE. Is it a fruit or a vegetable?

The confusion about 'fruit' and 'vegetable' arises because of the differences in usage between scientists and cooks. Scientifically speaking, the pumpkin is definitely a fruit. True fruits are developed from the ovary in the base of a flower, and contain the seeds of the plant (though seedless varieties may be cultivated): blueberries, raspberries, and oranges are true fruits, and so are many nuts. Some plants have a soft part which supports the seeds and is also called a 'fruit' though it is not developed from the ovary: the strawberry is an example.

As far as cooking is concerned, some things which are strictly fruits may be called 'vegetables' because they are used in savoury rather than sweet cooking: the tomato is technically a fruit but is often used as a vegetable, and a bean pod is also technically a fruit. The term 'vegetable' is more generally used of other parts of plants, such as cabbage leaves, celery stalks, and potato tubers, which are not strictly the fruit of the plant from which they come. Occasionally the term 'fruit' is used for a part of a plant which is not a fruit, but which is used in sweet cooking: rhubarb, for example.

As it happens, pumpkin is no longer listed in the definition of 'vegetable' in the latest edition of the *Concise Oxford Dictionary*, but it is possible to regard it either as a fruit or a vegetable: it is the fruit of the pumpkin plant, but can be used as a vegetable in cooking.

Q I heard someone say on the radio that the banana is a herb, but the dictionary lists it as a fruit. Which is right?

Both are right. A banana (the yellow thing you peel and eat) is undoubtedly a fruit. However, the banana *plant*, though it is called a 'banana-tree' in popular usage, is technically regarded as a herbaceous plant (or 'herb') not a tree, because the stem does not contain true woody tissue.

Q Do you eat soup or drink it?

Either! It may depend on the soup: you may drink a clear consommé even if you use a bowl and spoon, but you may feel that you have to eat a thick soup full of large vegetable chunks, even if it is in a mug.

Q Can't we do something about the horrible use of HOPEFULLY as if it meant 'it is hoped', instead of 'full of hope'?

It is not possible for us or anyone else to lay down hard and fast rules for the use of English, and we must all learn to live with changes we deplore. Some uses of words are a pity: there is no need, for example, to use *regretfully* where *regrettably* would be correct. However, the language lacks a word *hopably* which could be used in the same manner as other adverbs such as *fortunately*, and the use of *hopefully* in this context is undoubtedly here to stay.

Many words now generally accepted were bitterly criticized in the past: the introduction of the word *reliable*, for example, caused a storm of contention, and whole books were written on the subject. Yet the word has become quite uncontroversial.

Q I still receive information about DIALLING telephone numbers, but I now have a push-button telephone, not the old-fashioned kind with a dial. Isn't this a misuse of the word? Shouldn't we now 'push-button' the number?

The use of the term **dial** for the action of making a telephone connection on a push-button phone is probably best regarded as a development rather than a misuse of the language, since it seems to be quite natural as an extension of the word's use, and is clear in meaning, with no alternative word readily available.

It is only by the constant extension of the meanings of words that language grows and adapts to changing circumstances. 'Dial', for example, originally meant 'a sundial'. In the 16th and 17th centuries it was extended to mean 'clock' (and we still use it to mean 'clock-face'), and then in the 19th century became applied to the round piece on the front of a telephone, and acquired a new use as a verb.

Similar technological introductions have resulted in the spread of the new use of the word **enter** as in 'entering data into a computer', and new combinations such as **key in** ('key in your personal number'); either of these may possibly take over from 'dial' eventually.

Q Is it right to say that telephone calls are answered IN ROTATION, even though each one is only answered once?

Logically speaking, telephone calls are answered 'in sequence', since 'rotation' strictly implies a *recurring* sequence. However, the phrase 'in rotation' is well established in the sense 'in turn, in succession', and so its use in this context would also be acceptable.

Q I've always understood that the verb corresponding to 'destruction' is 'destroy', but I recently saw the word DESTRUCT in print. Is this wrong?

The verb **destruct** does exist, and originated in the USA in the 1950s. It is used mainly in connection with missiles and rockets, and means 'destroy a rocket or missile deliberately, especially for safety reasons' or '(of a rocket) be destroyed in this way': the compound form **self-destruct** is perhaps better known. Although it is still rather new compared to *destroy* it cannot really be described as wrong: it is a back-formation from *destruction*, formed by analogy with *construct/construction*. In fact, even the verb **construct** was at one time a new-fangled coinage: it was first used only in the 17th century, the older verb corresponding to *construction* being *construe*.

Q People nowadays often use the phrase UNDER THE CIRCUMSTANCES but surely as 'circumstance' comes from the Latin *circum* meaning 'around', 'in the circumstances' is the only correct form.

This is a common misconception and Henry Fowler, in his book *Modern English Usage* (1926), gets quite heated on the subject.

> 'the circumstances' means the state of affairs, & may naturally be conceived as exercising the pressure under which one acts. *Under the circumstances* is neither illogical nor of recent invention (1665 in *OED*), & is far more often heard than *in the circumstances*. The *OED* . . . assigns them different functions: 'Mere situation is expressed by "*in* the circumstances", action affected is performed "*under* the circumstances".'

The advice, then, is that 'under the circumstances' is acceptable, and especially when it is an action that is being discussed.

The more general point illustrated by many of these letters is that the meanings and use of words do not depend on their ori-

gins, or on what their constituent parts mean or originally meant. To treat words in this way is like treating people as mere amalgams of their parents, but words, like people, are separate individuals and have to make their own way in the world. While some will stay quite close to their roots, others will end up completely different in meaning and function, and there is nothing that we or anyone can do to stop them.

Q The *Concise Oxford* marks GOTTEN as an American usage, but I am sure that Trollope uses it in his novels.

Trollope does indeed use the word **gotten**, and the use of this form of the past participle of **get** goes back a long way in British English. The spellings *goten* and *gotin* were in use from the 13th century onwards, and *gotten* is recorded from the late 15th century. However, the first edition of the *OED* declared in 1899 that the use of *gotten* was almost obsolete, except in dialect. A late British example may be found in John Buchan's *The Courts of the Morning* (1929). Buchan was a Scot, and the *English Dialect Dictionary* lists *gotten* as being common in dialects throughout Scotland, so perhaps his use is dialectal.

The word **gotten** can thus be seen to have been in regular use in Britain from medieval times until at least the 19th century. However, the *COD* is a dictionary of current English and **gotten**, though it has remained in ordinary use in North America, is no longer current in Britain, except in some dialects and in the phrase 'ill-gotten', and indeed is regarded by most British speakers as an Americanism of the first rank.

Q How may I correctly ask a question in English in order to get an answer which contains an ordinal number such as 'I am my parents' third son' or 'Lincoln was the sixteenth president of the United States'?

We are often asked this question, especially by Indian correspondents. There is no idiomatic way of asking a question of this kind. In colloquial speech one might say, 'What number president of the United States was Lincoln?', but this would not be acceptable in formal use. One must ask the question in an oblique way, such as 'How many presidents of the United States were there before Lincoln?', or 'Where does Lincoln come in the list of presidents of the United States?', or 'How many elder brothers do you have?'

Pronunciation *is a constant source of trouble, especially among avid listeners to the radio, and especially as accent in English is so often taken as a marker of social status or education. The peculiarities of English spelling do not help: written English is a kind of code which corresponds word for word, but not letter for letter, with the spoken language.*

Q Should I write 'an hotel' or 'a hotel'?

You should only write *an hotel* if you are one of the increasingly few old-fashioned people who actually say 'an 'otel', with a silent *h* on the unstressed first syllable. The use of *a* and *an* before consonants and vowels depends on the spoken word. So we write *an heir* saying 'an 'eir', and *an honour* saying 'an 'onour', but we usually write *a historian* saying 'a historian', and always write *a European* saying 'a Yeuropean'.

Q I was taught always to pronounce the 'h' sound in words spelt with initial 'wh-', such as 'where' and 'which', and told that to drop it was uneducated. Is the widespread use of a plain 'w' sound a mark of poor education or just carelessness? The *Concise Oxford Dictionary* seems to regard it merely as 'ordinary'.

At the time of compilation of the original *Shorter Oxford* in the late 1920s and early 1930s, the editors considered that the /hw/ was used by a large proportion, but not a majority, of educated speakers in England. *Everyman's English*

Pronouncing Dictionary (1989 edition) notes that the /hw/ pronunciation 'must be regarded as increasingly rare'. However, this comment does not apply to Scottish or Irish accents, which are characterized among other features by the retention of /hw/.

Both the *New Shorter* and the current *Concise* are intended to reflect contemporary 'Received Pronunciation' (RP, in its standard form, not the 'marked' upper-class form), and they give /w/ rather than /hw/ pronunciations. The use of /hw/ in most of England is now distinctly formal and old-fashioned, and though it may be used in public speaking and singing, its ordinary use by a younger speaker of English might well appear affected or pretentious. It is certainly not a mark of education; more one of regional origin or social background (or aspiration).

Many such features of pronunciation pass gradually up the social and educational scale until they become entirely universal. As well as the shift from /hw/ to /w/, twentieth-century English has seen a shift in several vowels. A notable shift is that from /ɔː/ to /ɒ/, so that *cross* no longer rhymes with *force* in common use, and Gilbert and Sullivan's long-drawn-out pun on *often* and *orphan* in *The Pirates of Penzance* sounds contrived to a modern audience. Another is that from /æ/ to /a/, so that radio announcers of the 1940s sound astonishingly 'posh', pronouncing words like *hat* almost as 'het'. (Old recordings of the choir of King's College, Cambridge, are also illuminating in this regard: 'My soul doth *megnify* the Lord'!)

Earlier shifts in pronunciation have become firmly established. We shall discuss *receive* and similar words in the context of spelling (p. 137): other words have clearly had different sounds in the past, and not all 'false' rhymes in the older poets are the result of poetic licence. This famous couplet rhymed perfectly well in the original:

> *Here, thou, great Anna! whom three realms obey,*
> *Dost sometimes counsel take—and sometimes Tea.* (*tay*)
> Pope, *Rape of the Lock* (1711)

Q I had assumed that 'impious', the opposite of 'pious', was pronounced like 'pious' with 'im-' before it (as in 'piety' and 'impiety'), the stress being on the second syllable, but the dictionary gives a pronunciation with the stress on the first syllable. Surely this is inconsistent?

The accepted pronunciation of **impious** does appear incongruous at first sight, but it is quite firmly established. There are a number of pairs of opposites which have similarly divergent pronunciations, notably *famous* and *infamous*, *finite* and *infinite*, and *potent* and *impotent*. In such cases, the positive and negative words have made their separate ways into English from Latin, and the negative word is so much used in its own right that it has been unaffected by the existence of the opposite. Some other words with a negative meaning have the same pattern of pronunciation, but no opposite in regular English use: examples include *impudent*, *indolent*, and *innocent*.

Perhaps the decline of piety has something to do with the growing unfamiliarity of the word **impious**, but it is now increasingly pronounced in the more obvious way, to match impiety, and this pronunciation is included as an alternative in the *New Shorter Oxford English Dictionary*. Some people are misled by the older pronunciation into thinking that the word means the same as *impish*, and to avoid such confusion the stress may in future move unequivocally on to the second syllable.

Q How would you pronounce DON QUIXOTE?

Like most dictionaries, the Oxford dictionaries usually prefer to give the Anglicized pronunciation /ˈkwɪksəʊt/ ('quicksote'). This matches the English adjective **quixotic**, and seems preferable to making an inaccurate stab at the Spanish ('ki-*h*oteay', with an un-English consonant) or quixotically attempting the French ('ki-shot').

Finally, just for completeness, here is a classic problem of ***punctuation*** *often raised by our correspondents:*

Q I was taught not to put a COMMA before 'and' in lists of words, but I have seen it in many books. Isn't it wrong?

People have different opinions about the use of a comma (a 'serial comma') before 'and' in lists, but it is the practice of the Oxford University Press to put one in (which is why it is sometimes called the 'Oxford' comma). In some cases it is actually necessary to make sense of the list. For example, this sentence would be tricky to read without the extra comma:

We went shopping at Woolworths, Marks and Spencer's, and Debenhams.

and so would this one:

The scarves on sale were black and pink, red and yellow, and blue and white.

In most contexts it is a matter of choice whether to use a comma or not, though if you do adopt the 'Oxford' comma it is best to do so consistently, to avoid appearing careless.

5

Is there a word . . .?

OWLS gets numerous enquiries which begin, 'Is there such a word as . . .? It may be a word that the enquirer has seen or heard, or one that has been in the family for many years, but that is not in the enquirer's dictionary. The ***OED*** *is always our first resource; and we check all the likely alternative spellings or forms, in case the word has been misspelt or misheard. Quite often, this is as far as we need to go.*

Q Is there such a word as EPISCOPICIDE?

Yes, but it is extremely rare. It means 'the murder of a bishop' and in this sense we know of no instances of its use after the middle of the 18th century. It is marked *obsolete* in *OED*, but we have in our files a quotation from the early part of this century in which it is used humorously for something fatal to bishops; it recommends laying down episcopicide to keep them away.

Q When as a child I used the word AIN'T, my mother tried to discourage me by saying 'ain't ain't in the dictionary, ain't ain't'. Is it?

Yes it is, as a contraction for 'am not', 'is not', 'are not', 'has not', or 'have not'. Writers such as Dickens and Mark Twain have put the word in the mouths of their characters, and it was also used as a rather affected colloquialism by the British upper classes, although this is seldom heard nowadays.

Whether you should use it or not is another matter. The *Concise Oxford Dictionary* gives the following warning: 'Usually regarded as an uneducated use, and unacceptable in spoken and written English, except to represent dialect speech.'

Q In an old book I came upon the word OECONOMY. It seems to mean more or less the same as 'economy', but is there such a word?

This is an older form of the word **economy**, in use up until the 19th century, and reflecting the word's derivation from Latin *oeconomia*, Greek *oikonomia*. *Oe* was the usual Latin spelling of Greek *oi*. **Ecology** and **ecumenical** have a similar history: both once began with an *o*.

In most words Latin *oe* representing Greek *oi* has now become *e*. The exceptions are proper names, such as **Oedipus**, and some technical and medical terms. The former probably will not change but the latter may well do so. Words such as **oestrogen, oedema, apnoea,** and **diarrhoea** are spelt without an *o* in American English; **fetus** (which is from Latin, not Greek) is now the preferred spelling in British medical circles, although **foetus** is still commonly used. (The use of *ae* and *oe* is also discussed on pp. 139–40.)

Q My neighbour uses 'tixotropic' as a swear word 'because it sounds so nice and it's not rude'. She is sure she's seen it somewhere, but we cannot find it in the dictionary. Has she made it up?

If my guess is right the word she means is **thixotropic**, an adjective used to describe a gel which turns liquid when shaken or stirred, but returns to a gel when left to stand. It is often seen on tins of non-drip paint.

Q Is there such a word as PATAPHYSICAL, or is it a misprint for *paraphysical*?

The word **pataphysics** was invented by the French 'absurdist' writer Alfred Jarry (1873–1907) as the name of a notional branch of learning additional to metaphysics.

The word **metaphysics** itself is rather odd in its history. The works of Aristotle on theoretical philosophy were known in medieval Greek as *Metaphusika*, derived from the Greek phrase *ta meta ta phusika* 'after the Physics', which seems simply to have described where they came in the collected works of Aristotle. **Pataphysics** is explained as being from the phrase *ta epi ta metaphusika* 'the (works) imposed on the Metaphysics': no actual subject-matter seems to have been envisaged by Jarry.

Paraphysical also exists, and (like **parapsychology**) is derived from another Greek stem, *para*, meaning 'beside, beyond, to one side, irregular'. It is used mainly to describe physical phenomena for which no adequate scientific explanation currently exists.

Q I've been reading the novel *Family and Friends* by Anita Brookner. In the last chapter she uses the word LUDIC, which I cannot find. My wife claims this is just another example of Ms Brookner's imagination.

Ludic is a term used in psychiatry and psychology to refer to undirected and spontaneously playful activity—**ludic activity** is what we would call 'play'. It is now occasionally used outside the profession, but my guess is that it sounds too much like **ludicrous** (to which it is distantly related) to come into general use.

A particular source of curiosity are those words which, it seems, ought to exist.

Q Is there an adjective derived from integrity? I think I remember coming across INTEGRITOUS, but it does not appear in the dictionary.

There is an unfortunate lack in the vocabulary of English here, and a word would seem to be needed. The word **integritous** has indeed been used. However, the only examples we have are from the Kai Lung stories of 'Ernest Bramah' (Ernest Bramah Smith, 1869–1942), which are written in a convoluted mock-serious and supposedly Oriental style which is very funny to read but does not provide a very sound basis on which to assess English usage.

The source of the English word **integrity** is the Latin word *integritas*, which is derived from a Latin adjective *integer* meaning 'whole, entire, intact' (hence the mathematical term **integer** for a 'whole' or non-fractional number). One 17th-century author therefore logically used **integer** as an adjective to go with **integrity**, but this use did not catch on. The Latin *integritas* passed into Old French as *entièreté*, from which we get our word **entirety**, so, from the historical point of view, another possible alternative to **integritous** is **entire**. This word was indeed so used from the 15th to the early 18th centuries (variously spelt): 'Some very honest and intire Men . . .' (Edward, Earl of Clarendon, *The History of the Rebellion and Civil Wars in England*, 1647). To revive this use, though, would probably be difficult in modern English. Perhaps **integritous** may yet come into ordinary use, but anyone using it at present is likely to receive a funny look.

Q Is there such a word as KILTER? If not, how can anything be out of it?

Kilter (also spelt **kelter**) has existed since the 17th century, although we do not know its origins. It was widespread in

English dialects, and was also used in the USA, before becoming accepted as standard English. Nowadays it is almost always used in the phrase **out of kilter,** meaning 'out of order, not in good condition', but formerly it also applied to good health or spirits and was used in the phrases *in* (*good*, *high*, etc.) *kilter* and *get into kilter* as well as **out of kilter**.

Kilter is also a word for a hand consisting entirely of cards of low value—the holder might not be out of kilter but might well be out of the game.

Q If 'Disgusted of Tunbridge Wells' ever cheered up, would he find himself GUSTED?

He might, but if he was aware of it he would feel safer keeping the knowledge to himself. **Disgust** derives ultimately from Latin *gustus* 'taste' (via older French *desgouster* (now *dégoûter*) or Italian *disgustare*). *Gusted* therefore meant 'having a particular taste', and was used with adverbs such as 'well' and 'sweetly'.

Q Does the word 'WIELDY', the opposite of 'unwieldy', exist? It seems a useful word, and I'll be gruntled if it does.

The word **wieldy** certainly exists. The *Concise Oxford Dictionary* defines it as 'easily wielded, controlled, or handled'. Up until the late 17th century it was also used to mean nimble, agile, or vigorous. *Wieldable* and *wieldsome* were short-lived alternatives.

Gruntled also exists, although it has changed its meaning. **Disgruntled** comes ultimately from the verb *gruntle*, which originally meant to make a little grunt, like a small pig, and in the late 16th century meant to grumble or complain. **Dis-** in this case is used to intensify a word which already has a negative meaning, so *gruntled* in effect, would have meant the same, but not quite as bad, as **disgruntled**. However, we know of only one example of *gruntle* in this sense in the last three hundred years. **Gruntled** has since been reinvented as the opposite of **disgruntled**, and this is how it is used today.

The first example we have, and the most widely known, is from P. G. Wodehouse:

> He spoke with a certain what-is-it in his voice, and I could see that, if not actually disgruntled, he was far from being gruntled.

The invention of a word from another word that would appear to be derived from it is by no means unusual; the technical term for it is *back-formation*. Words formed from their apparent opposites include **couth** from **uncouth,** possibly **kempt** from **unkempt,** and **ept** from **inept**. The former is much like **gruntled** in that **couth** is a reinvention. The original word was an adjective from Old English *cunnan* 'to know', and was used in various senses of 'known', from familiar to famous, up until about the early 17th century. It survived in Scots as **couth** or **couthie,** meaning friendly or kindly, behaving as one would to an acquaintance or friend rather than to a stranger. **Uncouth** was used in various senses of 'unknown', from uncertain to unaccustomed and unfamiliar; its range of meanings included remote and desolate, foreign, and strange—from there it was only a short step to uncultured, awkward and clumsy, the predominant sense today, and the one that has given rise to the 'new' word **couth**. (**Outlandish** also shows a progression from 'foreign' to 'bizarre': in Coverdale's translation of the Bible King Solomon loved 'outlandish' women, in the King James version they are 'strange'. The context makes it clear that they were from other tribes rather than being odd.)

It is difficult to say for certain whether **kempt** is a survival or a back-formation. The root word is the Old English verb *cemban,* largely replaced by the related word **comb**. *Kembed* or *kempt* meant 'combed' and were sometimes used with adverbs such as 'well' and 'neatly'. There is a huge gap in evidence for either word between the early 17th and mid-19th centuries, and in the meantime **unkempt** and the earlier form *unkembed* had come to mean scruffy and neglected. In modern use **kempt** means the opposite of this, rather than 'combed'.

By contrast, **ept** is a pure back-formation; it did not appear in English until the mid-20th century, some 400 years after its source. **Inept** is from Latin *ineptus* meaning 'unsuitable, tasteless, silly'; it is related to **apt**. The negative prefixes **in-**, **de-**, or **dis-** existed in Latin and Old French, and many words beginning with them came into English as negatives. Often the corresponding positive came from the same source at about the same time, and it is both difficult and irrelevant to say which came first.

Old French *deschevele*, literally 'stripped of hair', gave us English **dishevelled**, meaning 'without a head-dress, with the hair loose', and later 'uncombed, untidy'. To our knowledge no one has invented the positive counterpart; if anyone wants to the correct form would be *shevelled*. However, **dishevelled** has given rise to a backformation: the verb **dishevel**. Just as we tend to think that if there is a negative there must be a positive, we assume that if there is a noun or adjective there must be a related verb, and if there isn't we invent one. Hence we get **laze** from **lazy**, **televise** from **television** and **burgle** from **burglar**; the American form **burglarize** is perhaps more logical but has not caught on here. We were recently asked whether there was such a word as *chiropodize* meaning to treat ailments of the feet, to which we replied that we have never met it, chiropodists don't use it, but there is really no reason why it shouldn't exist.

If the word is new, examples of it, collected by our team of readers, may be in our corpus or in our collection of quotations, awaiting the attention of the New Words department. If the New Words team are already working on the word in question we may be able to provide some information about it, although not a full and authoritative account.

Q I have been using the word 'humungous', but when challenged to prove that it exists, I was unable to do so. Is there such a word?

Yes, the word **humungous** does exist, but is of recent American origin and has not yet appeared in British dictionaries. It means 'extremely large', and seems to have been put together from parts of other words, such as 'huge' and 'monstrous', in such a way as to suggest words like 'tremendous' and 'enormous'. The earliest printed reference so far traced is in a list of American slang terms dated 1970, so it was presumably in use a little before then.

The word appears in our dictionaries as ***humongous****, as this proved to be the more common spelling;* ***humungous*** *is given as a variant.*

Some words are used only in dialect, in a particular trade or profession, in the terminology of a particular pastime, or the slang of a small section of the community. We have a large collection of reference books covering all sorts of topics, from boxing to heraldry, astrophysics to plumbing, children's games to botany, as well as dictionaries in most languages and of most varieties of English, from Old English to the present day, from Newfoundland to New Zealand, from 17th-century criminals' slang to computer jargon.

Q An engineer of my acquaintance recently used the words STICTION and SKY-HOOKS when talking about his work. Do these words exist, or was he trying to 'blind me with science'?

Stiction comes from 'static' and 'friction' (probably influenced by the verb 'to stick') and means static friction, the friction which tends to prevent stationary surfaces from being set in motion. The word **sky-hook** can be used for a contrivance for lifting, but is most often a piece of wishful thinking; a sky-hook being an imaginary device for attaching something to the sky or suspending something in the air. Faced with a completely impractical design for a tall structure or an aircraft an engineer may well ask the designer, 'How is it going to stay up, then? Sky-hooks?'

It helps if enquirers give us plenty of information about where, when, and in what context they came across the word—a photocopy of the item concerned, with the title and the date and place of the publication, is ideal, but any information is better than none. A simple 'is there such a word as . . .?' leaves us faced with hundreds of possibilities; 'I heard it from my grandfather, a Cornish fisherman who was born in 1880' will at least eliminate skateboarders' slang or post-structuralist literary criticism.

Q I am interested in the word JILLPOKE, which I learned from my mother (b. 1908). It refers to the situation when something has become wedged between the back and the surround of a drawer: 'the drawer won't open, there's something jillpoked in it' or 'a knife is (or has) jillpoked in this drawer'. I have only ever heard it used in our family, although my mother says that it was familiar to one other person, like herself a teacher and a native of New Brunswick. Can you tell me anything more about this useful word? Has it ever been used outside this very limited circle?

As you have found, there is no entry for **jillpoke** in the *OED* and we have no examples of it in our files. However, I have found reference to the word in the *Dictionary of Canadianisms on Historical Principles* (published by W. J. Gage Ltd. of Toronto). It seems to be confined to the lumber industry, and its origin is unknown. In British Columbia a **jillpoke** (or **gilpoke**) appears to be a pole driven into a river-bed to stop a raft of logs going aground or catching against the bank; in the Maritime Provinces it referred to a log with one end jammed into the bank and the other sticking out into the river (and no doubt snagging other logs). It has also been used to refer to a wagon with a broken shaft which has been run into the ground. There is no reference to either of the senses you mention, but both are presumably related to the 'jammed' sense.

*The extension of the 'jammed log' to recalcitrant cutlery struck one of our editors as a stroke of genius, and she has been using **jillpoke** in this sense ever since. Perhaps in years to come OWLS will receive an enquiry about it, saying, 'I learned it from my great aunt, born in the London area in the 1940s', and we will be totally misled.*

Word games give rise to many queries about the existence of words, some in terms that suggest that the game ended acrimoniously.

Q We were playing a game in which one player thinks of a word and the others have to find out what it is by asking questions. One player chose ZIMBABWE, which of course we didn't get because it's a proper noun, which is not allowed. He insists that it's an ordinary noun which he's seen in an English dictionary, and he now refuses to play with us.

Zimbabwe is a common noun, although far from common in use. It is an African word meaning a walled grave, and is the name given to the numerous ruined medieval settlements which are found in the state of Zimbabwe and also in neighbouring countries. It appears in the *OED* and the *New Shorter Oxford English Dictionary*, and in historical and archaeological texts, but I have not found it in other English dictionaries.

You could argue that, as a 'foreign' word, referring to something specifically African, this is not acceptable. However, there are many similar words which are now more or less accepted into English. For example, **pizza** is an Italian word for an Italian food, and we have adopted both together. If you wish to buy or order one, there is no other word for it, just as there is no other word for a zimbabwe.

Q I put down the word THORNIER in a game of Scrabble, but was told that there was no such word because you could only put '-er' on words of one syllable. We could not find 'thornier' in our dictionary so I had to withdraw it, but I'm sure I've seen it.

I'm sorry you had to withdraw **thornier** as it certainly exists; I do hope it wasn't on the triple word score.

Single-syllable words almost always use the suffixes *-er* and *-est* in the comparative and superlative forms; words of three or more syllables use more and most. Two-syllable words vary. Adverbs ending in *-ly* use *more* and *most*, and so do adjectives formed from the participles of verbs (**boring, excited**) and many which already end in a suffix (**childish, harmless**). However, adjectives ending in the suffix *-y* can add *-er* or *-est*, the *y* changing to an *i*, so **thornier** and **thorniest** are quite correct. The rules concerning the comparative and superlative, with associated spelling changes and more examples, can be found in the *Oxford Guide to English Usage*.

You might find that a dictionary that gives the comparative and superlative forms of adjectives and adverbs, and also the past tenses of verbs, would save a lot of argument. The *Concise Oxford Dictionary* does so, and is also of a good size and scope for word games. (It also contains American spellings, so you would have to agree in advance whether to allow them.) However, it really does not matter very much which dictionary you use—provided, of course, that you all use the same one.

Q One of the clues in a crossword read 'troops in charge emerge from a colonnade'. It was obviously an anagram of 'troops in'; other answers gave me the position of some of the letters, and I ended up with the word 'portino'. As it was such an unfamiliar word I looked it up in my dictionary, but could not find it. Does it exist?

We don't think so. We think that the answer was an anagram of *troops* plus *i* and *c* from 'in charge', and the answer was **portico.**

Many enquiries about the existence of words begin, 'Is there a word for . . .', and these are much more difficult to answer. Dictionaries are not designed to answer this question, and it would be very difficult to produce one in book form that did, although the ***Reader's Digest Reverse Dictionary*** *is good within its limited scope. The answer to a question such as 'what is the correct term for the part of a suit of armour that protects the knee' will be found in a book about armour rather than in a dictionary (the word is* ***poleyn****). Sometimes, however, the textbooks leave us little the wiser:*

Q What is the correct term for a BABY HEDGEHOG?

There does not seem as yet to be an established word for a baby hedgehog, and most books about mammals speak only of 'baby' or 'young' hedgehogs. The word **kit** is occasionally used, but there is as yet little evidence of its acceptance.

We do have in our files one example of the word **hoglet,** which appeared recently in the *University of Oxford Botanical Garden News*. This may well be a recent coinage, and certainly seems appropriate.

One side-effect of computerization has been the ability to give more satisfactory answers. At one time the request for a word meaning 'rain falling from a cloudless sky' might have defeated us, but we were able to answer it quite easily by asking the computer to search for the key words ***rain*** *and* ***cloudless*** *in one definition (the word was* ***serein****).*

Q Is there a word meaning the opposite of NOCTURNAL?

Yes: it is **diurnal**, used to describe an animal that is active during the day. The same word is also used to mean 'occurring every day' or 'daily', as in the phrase 'diurnal rhythm'. There is also a word **crepuscular** used to describe animals which are active during twilight.

Q I have discovered the word 'uxoricide', which means 'wife-killer'. Is there a word which means HUSBAND-KILLER?

No, husband-killing does not seem to have been given the status of a word to itself, despite the numerous husband-killers of history and legend, and it falls under the general heading of **parricide** 'murder of a close relative (not necessarily a father)'. The word **viricide** (from Latin *vir* 'man, husband') was once used by an 18th-century poet, but in modern use this word would be understood as referring to a substance for killing viruses. If a word for 'husband-killer' seems necessary, it would be possible to coin something like *mariticide* from another Latin word for 'husband'.

*Diurnal was found simply by asking the computer for **active** and **day**, and **crepuscular** by using **active** with **twilight**; had this drawn a blank then near-synonyms such as **dusk** and **evening** would have been tried. **Viricide** was actually defined as 'the slaying of a man or husband'. While the combination of **murder** and **husband** would not have found it, **husband** is not a common word in definitions, and searching for **husband** alone gave us a manageable list of words to check.*

Sometimes a search will reveal closely related words, although not the one in question.

Q Can you please tell me the word for the smell of blackened toast? I'm sure I came across it many years ago; I think of it every time I burn the toast but I just cannot remember what it was.

I regret I am unable to trace a word referring just to this specific smell. The nearest appropriate word is **empyreuma,** the burnt smell imparted to any organic substance (including toast) by the action of fire. Burning bacon, however, emits a **nidor,** as do all animal substances when cooked.

But the computer can only answer the question we ask; it does not know what we mean. If each of the key words in a definition has several near-synonyms it would take too long to search all the possible combinations. We often have to rely on our own (collective) knowledge of English and foreign words, Greek and Latin roots, word origins, word formation, history and literature, making an educated guess at what the word might be, and then checking to see if it exists.

Q I've been trying to think of a word meaning to attribute animal behaviour and characteristics to humans, a sort of reverse of anthropomorphize. Is there such a word?

There is no word in common use. **Zoomorphize** means to attribute an animal form or nature to someone or something, but usually refers to superhuman beings such as the animal-headed gods of ancient Egypt. Other possibilities are **animalize,** which can mean to make someone into an animal or to represent someone or something in animal form, but is more often used to mean to reduce to the level of an animal, or to rouse the animal passions of, and **bestialize,** which means to change into the form or nature of a beast, to brutalize or debase in character. Both of these assume that animal characteristics are negative or inferior to human ones; **zoomorphize** is the only one you could use in a neutral or positive way.

Q I have recently come across the word SESQUICENTENARY for a 150th anniversary, but I have been unable to

find a word for a 250th anniversary. Is it 'sesquibicentenary'?

No, this word is not in established use, and does not fit with the way that the prefix *sesqui-* has usually been used. Although logically it means 'and a half', this prefix has historically been used to form words referring to mathematical ratios relating a number to the next lower number (3 to 2, 4 to 3, 5 to 4, etc.).

The first ratio in the series is 3 to 2, and the name **sesquialtera,** sometimes seen applied to an organ stop, refers to two rows of pipes having lengths in this ratio. A ratio of 3 to 2 is the same as the ratio of 1½ to 1, so the prefix *sesqui-* is used on its own to mean 'one and a half times', but the next in the series, **sesquitertial,** means not 'three and a half times' but 'in a ratio of 4 to 3 (or 1⅓ to 1)'.**Sesquiquartal** similarly refers to a ratio of 5 to 4 (or 1¼ to 1), **sesquiquintal** to one of 6 to 5, and so on. On this basis, a 'sesquitercentenary' would presumably therefore be a period of one and a third centuries, i.e. a 133rd anniversary. A **sesquibitertial** ratio is one of 1⅔ to 1 (or 5 to 3), which would make a 'sesquibitercentenary' a 167th anniversary. Extending the analogy, a 'sesquibicentenary' would be 'one and two halves of a century', which is the same as 'two centuries'. Two hundred and fifty years is 'one and three halves of a century' (or 5 to 2), but there isn't a word for this ratio, and 'sesquitrialteral', though logical, would be very confusing.

Despite this, it is a pity that *sesqui-* does not mean simply 'and a half'. Since it comes from the Latin *semi-* 'half' and *-que* 'and', to use it in this way would be reasonably logical, if unhistorical. The word *quasquicentennial* has been invented for a 125th anniversary (based rather irregularly on the Latin *quadrans* 'quarter'), and *sesquibicentenary* is no less logical.

Meanwhile, our best suggestion for a 250th anniversary is **semiquincentenary,** formed by analogy with the existing word **semicentenary** for a 50th anniversary. This theoretically allows for unwieldy higher equivalents such as **semiseptcen-**

tenary (350th) and **seminongenary** (450th). The word **nongenary** (900th) is the only etymologically correct form for a 'higher centenary' which has passed into regular use: **quadringenary** (400th), **quingenary** (500th), **sescenary** (600th), **septingenary** (700th), and **octingenary** (800th) were also suggested by Henry Fowler in *Modern English Usage* (1926) on the basis of the equivalent Latin words, but the usual terms are **quatercentenary, quincentenary, sexcentenary, septcentenary**, and **octocentenary**.

Q What's the female equivalent of the word BRETHREN?

Sistren, although the words have rather different histories and so are not precisely parallel. Both were used in Middle English (12th to 15th centuries) simply as plural forms of **brother** and **sister**. From about 1600 **brothers** began to take over from **brethren** (Shakespeare uses both), but **brethren** was retained to refer to fellow members of a religious community, profession, or society. Except for a few specialized uses, such as the Plymouth Brethren, its use even in these contexts is now often archaic or humorous. **Sistren** had fallen out of use completely by about the middle of the 16th century. It has recently been revived, mainly by feminist writers, and may regain general acceptance.

Q I think I once came across a word for the ability to make unexpected discoveries, but I can't remember what it was.

You are probably thinking of the word **serendipity**. This means 'the (supposed) faculty of making useful discoveries while looking for something else'. It refers to the story of *The Three Princes of Serendip*, translated from Persian into Italian in the 16th century, and then into English in several versions, one by Elizabeth Jamieson Hodges (1965) bearing the above title. Serendip is an old name for the island of Sri Lanka.

The word was coined by Horace Walpole. As he explained in a letter of 28 January 1754, the heroes of the story 'were always making discoveries, by accidents and sagacity, of things they were not in quest of'. The historian S. E. Morison remarked that the greatest serendipity of history was that which resulted in the discovery of America by explorers who were really looking for the Indies.

Q It is common for jokes to be made about foreigners, but the word 'xenophobia' (hatred or fear of foreigners) doesn't seem to be the right word to describe this. Is there a suffix meaning 'making fun of'?

There is no accepted suffix meaning 'mocking' or 'making fun of'. However, derogatory names for foreigners or jokes about foreigners have been called *ethnophaulisms* (from the Greek *phaulisma* 'disparagement, contempt'). This might form the basis of a series of related words of more specific application: e.g. *Hibernophaulisms* for Irish jokes.

The late Michael Flanders noted that Greek **xenos** *meant 'guest' as well as 'stranger, foreigner'—which led him to define xenophobia as 'hatred and fear of guests'. He was also responsible (with Donald Swann) for the song which gave rise to the following question.*

Q The song called, I believe, 'Have some Madeira, m'dear', by Flanders and Swann, describes the seduction of an innocent girl by an old rogue. It contains the line 'he put out the cat, the wine, his cigar and the lamps'. Later she 'lowers her standards by raising her glass, her courage, her eyes and his hopes' and later still she 'made no reply, up her mind, and a dash for the door'. Is there a technical term for such a figure of speech?

The word **zeugma**, literally 'yoking' from Greek *zeugnunai* 'to yoke', applies to a figure of speech in which a single word is made to refer to two or more words in a sentence, especially when applying to them in different senses. **Syllepsis** (from Greek *sullepsis* 'taking together') refers to a word being made to cover two or more functions in the same sentence, while agreeing with only one of them grammatically, or made to apply to two or more words in different senses.

As might be expected from our correspondents, the correct terms for figures of speech or what can only be described as linguistic curiosities constitute a popular subject.

Q What is the name given to words which have opposite meanings according to the context? I mean things like 'with', which actually means 'against' in 'fight with someone', or 'take action', which can mean to go on strike.

There does not seem to be an accepted term for these words, perhaps because there are not many of them. The word **autoantonym** has been suggested, from **auto-** meaning 'self' plus **antonym**, a word opposite in meaning to another. Others have called them **Janus words**; Janus was an ancient Italian deity depicted as having two faces, one looking forward and the other backward. In the Roman Empire his image was often placed over doors and gateways, which can let people in or keep them out, and his name is occasionally given to things with two different functions or that work in two different ways.

Q Is there a term for expressions like 'abso-bloody-lutely'?

The word is **tmesis**, originally a Greek word meaning 'a cutting', from *temno* 'to cut'. The dictionary definition is 'the separation of parts of a compound word by an intervening word or words'. In the 16th and 17th centuries this figure of speech was also called *diacope*, from the Greek word for a cleft or gash.

Q What is the word for a sentence containing all the letters of the alphabet, and are there any which use each letter only once?

Sentences containing all the letters of the alphabet are known as 'pangrams'. Very few have ever been constructed using only 26 letters. The 1991 edition of the *Guinness Book of Records* mentions: *Mr Jock, T.V. quiz PhD, bags few lynx.*

Several other 26-letter pangrams, all of them rather unintelligible, are given in the *Oxford Guide to Word Games* by Tony Augarde. This book has a whole section on pangrams, for those who are interested.

Q Is there a word for words which form a different word when spelt backwards?

We do not know of a word for this. A word (or group of words, or a number) which reads the same when spelt backwards (like *noon*) is a **palindrome**, so I suppose you could call words like *deliver/reviled* semi-palindromes or half-palindromes.

Relationships of various kinds also leave our correspondents searching for a word:

Q What is the opposite of MISOGYNY? I have found *misanthropy* in the dictionary but this does not seem to mean the right thing.

No, a **misanthrope** is a person who dislikes other people in general. The correct term for dislike of men in particular is **misandry**, and a 'man-hater' may be termed a **misandrist**.

The distinction is often drawn in word-formation between the two Greek words *anthrōpos* 'human being' and *anēr* (stem *andr-*) 'man, male adult'. For example, **anthropogenic** is applied to human origins, or to things originated by humans;

androgenic is applied to the male sex hormones. A similar distinction can exist between the Latin words *homo* (stem *homi(n)-*) 'human being' (as in **homicide**) and *vir* 'male adult' (as in **virile**), though the distinction has often been blurred, and the Romance languages have words for 'adult male' derived from *homo* (e.g. French *homme*, Italian *uomo*).

The prefix **homo-**, as in **homogeneous** and **homologous**, is quite unrelated, being derived from the Greek word *homos* 'same'. It is sometimes combined (to the horror of linguistic purists) with words of Latin origin, as in **homosexual** (which means 'attracted to the same sex' not 'attracted to men').

Q I'm looking for a word that denotes all people but is not based on 'man' or 'human', which exclude women.

It is unfortunate that the Germanic root of man means both 'human being' and 'adult male', so that women may sometimes seem excluded. In words like **mankind** and phrases such as **the origin of man** the meaning is clearly 'people' rather than 'adult males'. In some dialects and regional forms of English **man** is used to address any person. However, in recent years it has become less acceptable to use **man** for **person** in some contexts, especially if there is an available alternative. For example, **chairwoman, chairperson,** and even **chair** are now often heard alongside or instead of **chairman**. (There is no truth in the ingenious theory that **chairman** is derived from the Latin *manus* 'hand', because the chairman 'handles' the meeting.)

As alternatives to **man** or **mankind,** or the newer **humankind** (or the rather horrid **personkind**), we can only suggest some semantically related words which may be suitable in some contexts: folk, mortals, individuals, persons, people, the world, the population, everyone.

It is perhaps worth saying that the word **person** has nothing to do with **son**. It is derived from the Latin word *persona*, which was applied to the classical actor's amplifying mask, from *per* 'through' + *sonare* 'to sound'. Nor does the word

human contain the word **man,** being derived from a Latin adjective related to *homo*, which though it is used for 'male person' has the primary meaning 'human being'.

This debate about 'inclusive language' seems to have originated in the USA—whence also, paradoxically, the informal 'you guys' used to address a group of either sex or a mixed group. The new forms of 'chairman' and similar words did not meet with universal acclaim—some women had no objection to being referred to as 'chairman', while some chairpersons objected to 'chair' on the grounds that they were not pieces of furniture. Enquiries such as these reached a peak in the mid-1980s, and are now less frequent; perhaps the debate has served its purpose in raising public awareness of how language is used.

Q I have found myself stuck for a word to refer to my son's mother-in-law. Is there a word for the relationship between the respective parents of a married couple?

We know of no accepted term in English for a relationship between the respective parents of a married couple: Shakespeare did once use **brother-in-law** in this way (in *A Winter's Tale*, Act IV, scene 4), but the context is humorous and it was not a standard way of using the term.

A person who marries acquires a set of relations by marriage, but all such 'in-law' relationships relate directly to the couple, and no relationships between their wider families are recognized in the language. The phrase **-in-law** originally meant 'according to canon (Church) law', so that, for example, marriage between brother-in-law and sister-in-law is prohibited as if the two people in question were brother and sister. It was formerly used also for relatives now designated by **step-**, who also come within the prohibited 'degrees of affinity' for marriage. A person's children's parents-in-law do not in fact fall within the prohibited degrees (a woman may legally marry her son's wife's father), and so they are not strictly 'in-law' relations. This also accounts for the non-existence of terms such as **nephew-in-law**, since technically a woman may marry, say, the ex-husband of her niece.

It is usually necessary to refer to 'my son's parents-in-law' or 'my daughter-in-law's parents' or whatever, or simply use their names (though I have heard the term 'co-in-laws'). Words for relations acquired through a second marriage of one's parents are less rare, though, even so, few people bother to talk about half-uncles or step-aunts.

There may well be languages in which such words exist, just as there are some languages, for example, which distinguish between aunts as 'mother's older sister', 'mother's younger sister', 'father's older sister', 'father's younger sister', or have different words for 'half-brothers sharing the same father' and 'half-brothers sharing the same mother'. I know of no such complexities in any well-known European language.

Q Is there a recognized term for a person that one lives with and is committed to without actually being married?

There are several in use, but no one term that everyone feels comfortable with. **Boy-** or **girlfriend** are ambiguous and do not suit a committed middle-aged couple. **Common law husband** or **wife** is sometimes used; although it sounds very formal, such relationships are in fact not generally recognized in common law (though some recent legislation takes account of them), and some people feel that it implies that in some way they have neglected to marry, rather than making a conscious decision not to. **Live-in lover** seems to place the lover on par with a domestic servant who lives in, and in any case 'lover' suggests an adulterous and possibly ephemeral relationship. The Scots **bidie-in** and the American **POSSLQ** (person of opposite sex sharing living quarters) and **significant other** have not been adopted elsewhere. **Partner** is probably the most generally accepted term, and is defined in the *Concise Oxford Dictionary* as 'either member of a married couple, or of an unmarried couple living together'; but some people consider it too formal and businesslike for such an intimate relationship.

Why not just say 'the man (or woman) I live with'? Although it could imply that you simply shared accommodation with them, most people would understand it. Like 'partner' it suggests an equal and mutually beneficial relationship, and it is no longer than some of the alternatives.

Q Is there a word I can use to refer to my (numerous) nieces and nephews collectively?

In former times **cousin** was used much more loosely than it is now to refer to a range of relatives outside the immediate family, including nieces and nephews. Relatives of an older generation were called uncle or aunt, as they are today, but their children and grandchildren, and one's brother's or sister's children, could all be called cousins.

This meaning died out in about the 18th century, and although the current restricted usage is unambiguous, it does leave us without a collective term for nieces and nephews.

We get many enquiries about collective nouns—terms for a group of animals, birds, or people. Many are common, or at least fairly well known—a ***gaggle*** *of geese, a* ***flock*** *of sheep, a* ***pack*** *of wolves, a* ***school*** *of dolphins, a* ***pride*** *of lions. Others are more obscure—a* ***rag*** *of colts, a* ***kindle*** *of kittens, or a* ***pod*** *of whales, for example.*

Recent letters have asked for the correct terms for chickens (a ***brood*** *or* ***clutch*** *of newly hatched chicks, a* ***flock*** *of hens), goldfinches (a* ***charm****), pigs (a* ***herd****), snipe (a* ***wisp****), and swans (a* ***game*** *or a* ***herd****, or when flying a* ***wedge****).*

Collective nouns have always aroused interest, and over the years various lists and books of them have been published. One of the earliest is in the 15th-century ***Book of St Albans****, attributed to Dame Juliana Barnes, and many of her terms were taken* *up by 19th-century antiquarian writers and in historical novels such as Conan Doyle's* **Sir Nigel***, and are still published in modern dictionaries and books about words. Some of these terms are genuine and well-used, but many appear to have no existence outside the lists. The* **Oxford English Reference Dictionary** *contains a list of over a hundred of these words. Curiously, there are no established group terms for many common animals: a* **clowder** *of cats, for example, is listed in one or two 19th-century books, but we know of no genuine examples; it appears to be a dialect variant of* **clutter***.*

Two particular terms have become well known partly because they have been used as the titles of books: Ruth Rendell's **An Unkindness of Ravens** *and James Lipton's* **An Exaltation of Larks***, itself a collection of collectives. We are sometimes asked whether they are correct. We do not have any evidence that 'an unkindness of ravens' has ever been used in earnest. The complete* **Oxford English Dictionary** *does list* **exaltation** *with the obsolete sense 'a fanciful name for a flight of larks', but the first example is from a medieval list of collective names, the second is a piece of hearsay ('Every one with any pretence to be gentle-folk spoke of . . . an exaltation of larks'), and the third is rather negative ('I have never spoken of "an exaltation of larks"'). We know of no one who has genuinely used the word 'exaltation' when speaking or writing about larks.*

Collective names for kinds of people are scarcer in genuine use, and most are humorous, satirical, or punning: a **fawning** *of courtiers, a* **boast** *of soldiers (both of these from the 15th century), an* **exaggeration** *of anglers, a* **catalogue** *of librarians, a* **giggle** *of girls, an* **ambush** *of widows, an* **impatience** *of wives, an* **unhappiness** *of husbands (one suspects that misogynists have been at work here), a* **jam** *of tarts, a* **flourish** *or a* **blast** *of strumpets!*

We have been asked for terms for ex-wives (nothing officially recognized, but suggestions have included **string***,* **parade***, and, more poignantly,* **pain***) and for archdeacons. This last came from a church employee who had to arrange meetings of such dignitaries. The only term we could find in any list was* *__bundle__, but evidence for this is rather flimsy; we felt that it might be better to invent a more respectful term, and (since archdeacons are called 'the Venerable') suggested that __conveneration__ might be a possibility.*

We also receive many letters from collectors:

Q I have a large collection of (china cats / milk bottles / horse brasses / bus tickets / etc.). Is there a word for collecting these, or for a person who collects them?

'Probably not' is the most usual answer. Only the most well-established kinds of collecting have special names which can be regarded as truly in common use, such as **philately** (stamp-collecting), **numismatics** (the study and collecting of coins and medals), and **bibliophily** (book-collecting). People who collect bus tickets, theatre programmes, advertisements, greetings cards, calendars, and other printed or written items intended for short-term use are lumped together by the term **ephemerist** (from Greek *ephemeros* 'lasting only a day'). As far as we know there is no word for a person who collects 'collectables'. However, a number of other collecting hobbies have had mock-scholarly names devised for them which are occasionally seen in use, such as **arctophily** (teddy-bears, from Greek *arktos* 'bear'), **tegestology** (beer-mats, from Greek *tegestos* 'a small reed-mat'), **deltiology** (postcards, from Greek *deltion* 'a little writing tablet') and **copoclephily** (key-rings, from Greek *kope* 'handle' and *kleis* 'key'). Many of these words are only taken seriously, or even understood, by devotees of the hobby in question (and sometimes not even by them).

There are two sets of endings used to form words for collectors and collecting. One set is based on the Greek stem *-philos* 'loving' or its Latin equivalent *-philus*, which also form many technical words concerned with affinity or attraction. The English endings are **-phile** or **-philist** for the person, **-phily** or (sometimes) **-philism** for the action, and **-phile** or **-philic** for the adjective describing them. There can be a certain amount of ambiguity involved: **arctophile** means 'a person who likes and collects teddy-bears', but it could in theory be taken to mean 'a person who is sexually attracted to (real) bears'.

The other set is based on the Greek stem *-logos*, the basis of many names for branches of science and scholarship, and so words ending in **-logy** or **-logist** may imply a study of the thing collected rather than just a passion for collecting.

The main problem with modern words coined for collecting is the scarcity of suitable classical roots from which such terms could be derived. Some of the words proposed are extremely contrived: **infulaphily** (the collection of cigar-bands), for example, comes from Latin *infula*, which is here taken to mean 'a coloured strip', but in Latin usually meant specifically a woollen headband with knotted ribbons, or various other kinds of band connected with pagan ceremonies. **Fusilately** (the collection of phonecards or other plastic cards) seems to be based on Latin *fusilis* 'molten' (intended to express 'plastic') with the ending of **philately** (from Greek *ateleia* 'without charge', taken as implying 'pre-paid' or 'on credit'). A few are linguistically barbarous: **autonumerology** for an interest in car registrations is a misuse of *auto-*, which means 'self-', as if it were a prefix derived from **automobile** (which literally means 'moving by itself'); the proposed 'ornacatology' for the collection of ornamental china cats would make any philologist squirm.

To coin philologically acceptable words takes considerable thought, an acquaintance with classical languages, and access to dictionaries of Latin and Greek. It is our job as lexicographers to record and explain existing words, not to invent new ones, but occasionally the temptation cannot be resisted. One correspondent, for example, wrote to ask for a word for the collecting of bookmarks. The ancient Greeks did not have books in the modern sense, only scrolls, and had no word for a bookmark. However, there is a rare medieval Latin word *registerium*, which is applied to the coloured ribbon used to mark the place in a monk's service-book, so perhaps the

English word *registeriophily* could be coined. However, 'bookmark-collecting' seems perfectly adequate and easily understood. Another strategy is to use words from modern Greek, which provided the basis of the proposed terms *grabatophily* (tie-collecting, from Greek *grabata*) and *papigiology* (bowtie-collecting, from Greek *papigion*, itself from French *papillon*). Even this can sometimes fail to provide anything really usable: *elasticosphragidophile* is a bit of a mouthful for 'a rubber-stamp collector', though perhaps just *sphragidophile* would do (from *sphragis*, *sphragidos*: in modern Greek, a stamp, in ancient Greek, a signet-ring).

We always do our best to meet our correspondents' needs, and the wide variety of their interests and concerns is stimulating and, at times, challenging. However, sometimes not only the answer, but the reason for asking, escapes us:

Q Please can you tell me the word for a person who drinks their own bath-water, as opposed to one who drinks another's bath-water?

Despite concerted efforts we have been unable to discover any words for a person who drinks his own (or another's) bath-water. As the concept is not central to European civilization I am not surprised that it has failed to find a place in dictionaries. If words for this are needed in the future, then **autoloutrophilist** and **alloloutrophilist** are waiting in the wings ready for their brief flash of celebrity.

6

What does this mean . . .?

As a very ordinary member of the public I would like to know the full meaning of the following words.....
M.P.

The obvious answer to such a question would seem to be 'look it up in the dictionary', and sometimes, we confess, we get a little impatient when an enquiry can be answered simply by sending a photocopy from the ***OED****. However, we realize that not everyone has access to a big dictionary. We often get letters on prison notepaper; one enquired about the meaning of 'chloral hydrate' and 'Mickey Finn'—we did rather wonder why he wanted to know. We also had a letter from a lady claiming to be 'the wrong side of 80' (whichever side that is). She apologized for bothering us, as she had the compact version of the first edition and supplements, but by the time she had lugged it to the table and found her spectacles and her magnifying-glass, she tended to forget what she wanted to look up. And we know that some things do not appear in standard dictionaries, and some need a little more background information before they really make sense. So if people cannot find the information they want, we are always willing to help.*

Some of the words we are asked about are quite obscure, and we are not surprised that our correspondents have had difficulty tracing them:

Q I have come across the word TATTARRATTAT, said to be the longest palindromic (reversible) word in English. What does it mean?

This word, although it appears in the complete *Oxford English Dictionary*, is in fact not genuinely in accepted use. It was invented by James Joyce and used in his book *Ulysses* (1922), and is an imitation of the sound of someone knocking at a door.

Q What is the meaning of the word NEPHELOCOC-CYGEAL, which appears in my *Oxford Thesaurus*?

The word **nephelococcygeal** means 'of or relating to Cloud-Cuckoo-Land'. It is not in common use, but thesauruses often contain interesting or peculiar words which would not be admitted to ordinary small dictionaries. The expression 'Cloud-Cuckoo-Land' is in fact a literal translation of the Greek name *Nephelokokkygia*, so it is easy to see where the adjective comes from. Nephelokokkygia was a city built by the birds in the comedy called *The Birds* by the classical Greek comedy-writer Aristophanes.

Another word which is frequently found in thesauruses but not dictionaries is **apocolocyntosis**. This word was invented by the Roman author Seneca as the title of a satire mocking the Roman practice of deifying emperors. In the satire, the Emperor Claudius is refused entry to heaven. The word is a blend of the Greek words *apotheōsis* 'deification' and *kolokunthē* 'gourd': it is usually translated 'pumpkinification'!

Q I'm translating a book for children, but I have been unable to find meanings for the following words: ferisher,

shag-foal, grindylow, tantarrabobs. These are kinds of fairy, but it would be helpful to know exactly what they are so that I can translate them accurately.

According to *A Dictionary of Fairies* by Katharine Briggs:

Ferisher is a Suffolk name for fairies in general.

A **grindylow** is a Yorkshire water-demon who lurks in deep stagnant pools to drag down children who come too close to the edge.

Shag-foal is a Lincolnshire name for those spirits or bogies that change shape; they frequently take the form of a shaggy, fiery-eyed horse or foal.

A **tantarrabob** is a nursery word for a bogey or goblin; the sort of creature invoked to frighten children into good behaviour. In Devonshire dialect it is also used for the devil.

Q Can you please help me trace the meaning of the word CHAMINADE, which appears in *The Unbearable Bassington* by 'Saki' (H. H. Munro). I have looked in several dictionaries, both English and French, but have not found it. I also phoned the publisher, who very kindly offered to find the author's telephone number for me so that I could contact him direct: I thought this might be rather difficult as he died in the First World War!

Thank you for supplying us with a photocopy of the page; it makes our search so much easier if we know the context. On reading it I wondered if **chaminade** might be some kind of toilet preparation. The *Trade Marks Journal* of 1907 lists *La Chaminad* as a range of perfumery (including toilet articles, preparations for the teeth and hair, and perfumed soap) offered by Morny Brothers of New Bond Street. The entry has a few musical notes beside it, which may support my guess that there is some connection with Cécile Chaminade (1857–1944), a popular French composer of the day.

On one occasion we were able to contact the author direct. Having failed utterly to trace the word 'liggot', from a novel by Iris Murdoch, we asked the lady herself, who rather thought she had misremembered a dialect word for 'tied up'.

Other terms are everyday words to those in the know, and a complete mystery to everyone else.

Q I was listening to a programme on the radio where one of the speakers was talking about the game of cribbage, and mentioned what sounded like a 'pry-al'. Although I have played the game from time to time I didn't recognize the word. Can you help?

Prial is a variant spelling (and pronunciation) of the term **pair-royal**, used in various card games to denote a set of three cards of the same denomination. It can also be used of three dice which land showing the same number.

Q In my business I use large catering packs of flour, which have the word ENDOLETED on the label. I would very much like to know what it means.

You probably won't like to know; this is one of those occasions when 'ignorance is bliss'. Flour that has been **endoleted** has been spun in a large drum with ridges on the inside surface, in order to break up any insect eggs and prevent them hatching out while the flour is in storage. *Bon appetit!*

Q I have come across the word HIRSEL in a book about hill-farming. What is a 'hirsel'?

The word **hirsel** comes from the dialect of Scotland and the North of England, and is of Old Norse origin. Its basic meanings in English are 'the flock of sheep under a shepherd's charge' and 'the ground occupied by a flock of sheep'. Lord Home of the Hirsel took his title as a life peer from the name of his house near Berwick-upon-Tweed, which was presumably originally a place occupied by a flock of sheep.

Q Our daughter, who is horse-mad, has been begging us to buy her a pony. We are not 'horsey' people and we haven't anywhere to keep it. We explained all this to her, and after an initial sulk she said she would be content with a FALABELLA. We thought we had better find out what this is before we agreed!

A **falabella** is a very small breed of horse, originally bred by the Falabella family in Argentina. The maximum height is about 30 inches (76 cm), compared with 42 inches (107 cm) for a Shetland pony; they are also of a much lighter build. They can be ridden only by very small children and are usually kept as pets: they were very popular in the USA at one time. However, their needs are similar to those of any other kind of horse, and I doubt if one would fit happily into the average suburban semi. I believe they are also quite expensive to buy. I have great sympathy with your daughter, as I can remember similar conversations with my parents, but I would think very carefully before giving in.

Q I have recently found a bundle of 'letters home' written by my late uncle while he was in the Royal Navy between the wars. In one he says that he will soon be arriving in 'Guz' and will be on 'God's Wonderful' as soon as he gets leave. What did he mean?

He meant that his ship would soon be arriving at Devonport naval base and that he would catch the train from Plymouth as soon as he could. **Guz** is navy slang for Devonport; it may come from **guzzle** meaning 'liquor'—certainly one of the things sailors look forward to ashore. **God's Wonderful** is short for **God's Wonderful Railway**, an affectionate nickname for the old Great Western Railway, which served the south-west of England.

Q My young son has been a bit under the weather lately. The doctor took some blood for testing, and suggested that it might just be ossiloplombosis, although she didn't think so in my son's case. This isn't in our medical book, and I'm a little bit worried.

The word your doctor used sounds like **osciloplumbosis**, and if your son is suffering from it he may have more to fear from you than from the condition. This is a made-up, humorous word, from Latin *oscillare* 'to swing' and *plumbum* 'lead', with *-osis* denoting a process or condition. The doctor probably did not want to suggest in front of him that your son was malingering, or she may just have been joking.

A similar pseudo-medical term is **psychoceramic**, which translates roughly as 'crackpot'.

Even lexicographers can be guilty of confusing their readers . . .

Q I'd always called the word THE the definite article, but a recent dictionary calls it a DETERMINER. What does this mean?

A **determiner** is a blanket term for a word that limits or indicates the scope of a noun. It comes before the noun and any descriptive adjectives, and tells you whether the noun refers to a specific thing (and if so, which) or to that kind of thing in general. For example, in 'that book', 'his new coat', 'any time', and 'some boys', *that*, *his*, *any*, and *some* are determiners. Grammarians vary in how they use the term, but they usually include the articles (*a* and *the*), demonstrative adjectives such as *this* and *that*, possessive adjectives (*his*, *our*, *their*, etc.), and words expressing a quantity (*much*, *few*, *a lot of*, *several*, etc.).

'Foreign' words—words from other languages used in English, and English words used overseas—also cause problems. Even

everyday words used in an unexpected way can be completely mystifying, especially to those who speak English as a second, or even a third, language. We once received an enquiry from a Japanese gentleman who had been reading a book on Margaret Thatcher: 'Please,' he asked, 'what is handbagging?'

Q What are the meanings of the words (in Latin?) that appear around the edges of the pound coins?

There are three inscriptions round the pound coins, two in Latin and one in Welsh. Round the English (and Northern Irish) coin is *decus et tutamen*, a phrase from Virgil's *Aeneid* which means 'adornment and protection'. This phrase was originally inscribed on a shield presented to a victorious warrior. It was subsequently applied to the milling round coins, which both adorned them and, in the days when coins were made from precious metal, protected them from being filed down. The Scottish coin has *nemo me impune lacessit*, which means 'no one provokes me with impunity' and is a motto of the Order of the Thistle and of the Scottish kings. The Welsh coin has *pleidiol wyf i'm gwlad*, a line from the national anthem of Wales. It is translated as 'I am loyal to my country'.

Q When the Queen spoke of having an *annus horribilis* some people contrasted this with *annus mirabilis*. What does *annus mirabilis* mean?

Literally, a wonderful year, but it is often used more loosely to mean a remarkable or very eventful year.

Q What's the meaning of the words that appear on the coat of arms printed in Oxford University Press books?

The words—*Dominus Illuminatio Mea*—are the Latin motto of Oxford University. The motto means 'Lord, my enlightenment' and is taken from the first verse of Psalm 27 (26 in the traditional Latin Bible).

Q A friend who is visiting India has written saying she's bought me a SHALWAR KAMEEZ, which she is sure I will like. Will it go on the mantelpiece or should I clear out the shed?

The wardrobe would be the best place. A *shalwar kameez*, sometimes known as a shalwar suit, is a set of clothes worn by many Indian women, the *shalwar* being a pair of loose trousers and the *kameez* a long shirt or tunic.

Q I have been visiting relatives in Australia, and noticed that the newspapers often referred to things as CLAYTONS. What does it mean?

This modern Australian slang term originated as the name of a soft drink, which was publicized as 'the drink you have when you're not having a drink'. It is now widely used in Australia, especially in newspapers, to refer to something or somebody regarded as a sham or poor substitute ('the prime minister you have when you're not having a prime minister'), a soft drink presumably being regarded by most Australians as a poor substitute for a beer.

Q What is the meaning of 'rainmaker' and 'to take a raincheck', both of which I heard recently in an American film?

These are both terms which have a literal meaning, but are often used in a figurative or transferred sense. A **rainmaker** is a person who makes, or is believed to make, rain fall, either by magic or by scattering crystals on the clouds. In the USA, as in the UK, professional lobbyists try to infuence legislators on behalf of particular interest groups. In American political slang a very good lobbyist is sometimes called a rainmaker: someone who can produce results by apparently miraculous means.

A **rain check** is a ticket given to spectators at an event which has to be postponed or interrupted because of bad weather. It entitles the holder to a refund of the admission fee, or to readmission at a later date. It is also used for a ticket enabling a customer to reserve something which is not yet available, or to take up an offer at a later date. To **take a rain check (on)** means to reserve such a right, to postpone an appointment, or sometimes to stop an activity or discussion, with the intention of returning to it later.

As lexicographers we do not deal with proper names, except when they have become part of the language: names such as ***Shrapnel****,* ***Aunt Sally****, and* ***Banbury****, which will be included in the dictionary because of the things they refer to. However, names have their own meanings which we are sometimes asked about. Oxford University Press publishes various books on the names of people and places, although they are not produced in the dictionary department, and we can often find the answers.*

Q My son and daughter-in-law want to call their baby TIFFANY. I believe this is a jeweller's shop, and I don't really like the idea of my little granddaughter being named after it. Can you confirm this?

Tiffany & Co. is a firm of very high-class jewellers in New York, founded by Charles L. Tiffany. His son Louis became world-famous as an Art Nouveau decorator and designer, particularly noted for his iridescent glassware. The name **Tiffany** was given to glassware and lamps made in imitation of his style.

However, the origin of the surname may put your mind at rest. Originally this was a girls' name, *Theophania*, which became *Tiphaine* in French and *Tiffania* or *Tiphany* in English. It derives from the term used in the Orthodox Churches for the festival the Western Churches call Epiphany, held on 6 January to celebrate the manifestation of Christ to the Magi. The name was given to girls born on this day, and in medieval romances (never famed for their historical accuracy)

Tiphany became the name of the mother of the Wise Men. After the medieval period the name virtually died out, but survived in France as a surname. Its recent revival as a girls' name may owe something to the film of Truman Capote's novel *Breakfast at Tiffany's*.

Q Where on earth did the developers get the horrible modern name MILTON KEYNES from? Does it actually mean anything?

Milton Keynes was the name of one of the villages that was incorporated in the new town and, although for some reason it looks like a modern name, it is actually very old. **Milton** is a very common village name, of Anglo-Saxon origin. It usually means the middle farm or estate (Milton Keynes is mentioned in the Domesday Book as *Middeltone*) but sometimes refers to a settlement with a mill. **Keynes** comes from the Norman *de Cahaignes* family, who held the land in the 12th century.

Q What does STAN mean in names like Pakistan and Kazakhstan?

The suffix **-stan** means a province. Usually, as in Afghanistan and Kazakhstan, it signifies the province belonging to the tribe or people named. In the case of Pakistan, the country's name was made up from elements of the names of provinces, parts of provinces, or peoples included in it; *P*unjab, *A*fghan (a Pashto-speaking people living on the borders of Pakistan and Afghanistan), *K*ashmir, and Baluch*istan*.

Q I've been teased all my life about my name, RAMSBOTTOM. Please tell me it doesn't mean that!

As a surname it simply denotes a person from a place called Ramsbottom. As a place name, it may have one of several meanings. **Bottom** is quite straightforward, it comes from Old

English *botm* or Old Scandinavian *botn*, and means a broad river valley. **Ram** might refer to the animal or to the wild garlic plant (*hramsa* in Old English); it was also sometimes used as a nickname by the Anglo-Saxons. So **Ramsbottom** means (the settlement in) the valley where wild garlic grew, or where the ram was kept, or that was owned by a man known as Ram.

Q I'd always thought that the Saxon king Ethelred was called THE UNREADY because he was never ready to fend off the Danes, but I've been told that this is not true. If Unready does not mean 'unprepared' what does it mean?

Although modern spelling disguises it, the *red* of **Ethelred** and the *read* of **unready** represent the same word, the archaic English *rede*, meaning advice or counsel. The Anglo-Saxons used names made up of two elements, each of which had a meaning, although they often did not make much sense when they were put together. Ethelred's name meant 'noble counsel' and the epithet (*Unrede* according to later medieval writers) meant 'lack of counsel or wisdom, evil counsel, folly'. The whole name, therefore, is an early English pun; it means something like 'noble counsel uncounselled' and implies that he did not know how to deal with the Danes rather than that he was not ready for them.

Sometimes finding the answer is not just a matter of picking up the right reference book from the shelf:

Q Near where I live there is an estate which was built around the time of the present Queen's coronation, and all the roads are named after something to do with the ceremony or with heraldry: there is Orb Close, Sceptre Towers, Regal Road, Ampulla Road, Sovereign Road, Griffin Close, and lots more. Right in the middle is DYMOKE Road. It must

have something to do with the others, but although I've tried every dictionary and encyclopedia I can find, it really has me puzzled.

This one had me puzzled as well. I eventually found a full account of the Coronation service in a newspaper my mother had kept as a souvenir, and checked all the items and officials concerned. One was the 'Queen's Champion', and under the entry for **champion** in the *OED* I found the following quotation from *Cowel's Dictionary*, dated 1672:

> *Champion of the King*. His Office is at the Coronation of our Kings, when the King is at Dinner, to ride armed into Westminster-hall, and by a Herald make a Challenge, That if any Person shall deny the King's Title to the Crown, he is there ready to defend it; which done, the King drinks to him, and sends him a gilt Cup with a Cover full of Wine, which he has for his Fee. This Office ever since the Coronation of Richard the Second, hath continued in the Family of the Dymockes.

The Dymoke family, of Scrivelsby in Lincolnshire, still hold the office of Champion, although of course nowadays their duties are purely ceremonial.

Even the computer could not have helped us with this one, because of the different spelling of 'Dymoke'.

Many enquiries, however, concern everyday words and expressions, and often serve to remind us of our ignorance (probably no bad thing). They make us realize that, although the terms are familiar, we may not know precisely what they mean.

Q I've just bought a duvet which has a 'tog-rating' of 11.5. I know this is something to do with how warm the duvet is, but what is a TOG?

A **tog** is a unit of thermal resistance of fabric, technically the resistance that will maintain a temperature difference of

1 degree Celsius with a flux of 1 watt per square metre. In practical terms, one tog represents the insulation properties of a light summer garment and a 10-tog quilt is as warm as heavy winter clothing. The term probably comes from the slang word for clothes, **togs**, which itself comes indirectly from a 15th-century word *toge*, a loose coat or cloak, from Latin *toga*. Tog was coined by British clothing manufacturers, using the pattern of an earlier American unit, the *clo*; a tog is equal to 1.55 of a clo.

Q What does CORNED mean in corned beef? Is it a corruption of 'canned'?

No, it actually means preserved in salt; corned beef is cooked in salt before it is canned. The noun **corn** was once used for any sort of grain or particle, and many foods, particularly meat, were preserved by **corning**—sprinkling with grains of coarse salt.

Q If a building society gives me a mortgage on my house am I a MORTGAGEE, as I had supposed, or a MORTGAGOR, as the documents seem to imply?

To **mortgage** something means to make it over as security for a debt, so a householder who has mortgaged a house as security for a loan (often for the purchase of the house itself) is a **mortgagor**. The bank or building society is the **mortgagee**, that is, the person to whom the property is mortgaged. The mortgagor mortgages the property, and the mortgagee (or lender) lends the money in return.

Incidentally, **mortgagor** is one of the few English words in which a *g* followed by an *o* is pronounced soft, but the alternative spellings *mortgageor* and *mortgager* have not caught on.

Q If 'char' is another word for 'tea', does 'charwoman' mean 'tea-lady'?

No. **Char** meaning 'tea' comes from a Chinese word, and is related to the Russian word *chay*. This seems to be the word for tea that came overland through central Asia. **Tea,** on the other hand, comes from a coastal Chinese dialect (probably that of Amoy), and was transmitted by sea with the Malay and Portuguese traders.

The first syllable of **charwoman** is from the Old English word *cierran* 'to turn' (i.e. to do a turn of work), and is related to **chore**.

Q A police spokesman on the news last night, talking about a murder investigation, said that over 50 police were now involved in the EXERCISE. My dictionary says that an 'exercise' is something you do for practice—did he really mean that?

In its usual meanings **exercise** refers to an activity, a task or a set of tasks, with the implication of their being carried out to improve or maintain a skill, and like you I would hate to think that hunting murderers was something the police do just to perfect their technique.

However, in the phrase **the object of the exercise** the word does have the meaning of a procedure or activity undertaken with some purpose other than practice. For example, you have written to us, and the object of the exercise was not to hone your letter-writing skills. Having acquired this meaning within the phrase, **exercise** is now also being used in this way when standing alone or when followed by **in**. The meaning now seems to be firmly established, but because of the implication of practice or training that the word has, we need to be very careful of the context when using it in this sense.

Q What is an ANALOGUE watch? Is it something to do with the movement?

Analogue, applied to watches and clocks, concerns the method of showing the time. An analogue timepiece has a traditional face with numbers around the edge and hands, as opposed to a **digital** display where the time is shown in figures.

Before digital faces became popular there was no need for a term to describe an ordinary clock face. When the need for such a term arose it was borrowed from computing, where **analogue** was used to describe a system using physical variables, such as voltage, weight, or length, to indicate numbers, as opposed to a digital system which showed numbers as digits. On an analogue timepiece the numbers of hours and minutes are shown by the distance moved by the hands.

Q I've always known ANTIDISESTABLISHMENTARIANISM as a long word, but what does it actually mean?

It means the belief that the Church of England, the established Church, should not be 'disestablished', i.e. that the official link between Church and State should be maintained. Although discussion about whether or not this link should remain has been going on for over a hundred years, **antidisestablishmentarianism** is most often used merely as an example of a long word.

Q My fiancé has given me a gold pendant with an inscription which reads 'MIZPAH The Lord watch between me and thee when we are absent one from another'. What does MIZPAH mean?

Mizpah is a place name of Hebrew origin with the meaning 'a lookout or watch-tower'. It was the name given to a pillar or cairn of stones erected by Laban, the father-in-law of Jacob in the Bible. In Genesis 21: 48–9 Laban says, 'This heap is a witness between me and thee this day. Therefore was the name of it called . . . Mizpah; for he said, The Lord watch between me and thee, when we are absent one from another.'

Although it is often used as a token of affection between

lovers or friends, the biblical context is less happy. Jacob and Laban had fallen out, and Laban's words were a reminder to Jacob that God would witness any hostile action or any ill-treatment of Laban's daughters. Genesis 21 tells the whole story.

Q What is a 'runcible spoon', which the Owl and the Pussycat used in Edward Lear's poem?

This has been used to refer to a kind of pickle-fork, curved like a spoon and having three prongs, one of which has a cutting edge. However, this was later than the poem and not what Lear had in mind—his illustrations do not show anything like it, and he also used **runcible** to describe other things, including a cat, a hat, and a wall. **Runcible** seems to be just a word Lear made up, without any particular significance. It may be based on **rouncival**, which has had various meanings including 'gigantic', 'a monster', 'a wart', 'a large and boisterous woman' (all obsolete by Lear's time), but is most commonly used in the names of several plants of the pea family. Why he chose this word is not known—he probably just liked the sound.

Q I get very confused about the word INFLAMMABLE. Does it mean 'liable to catch fire' or the opposite?

It means 'easily set alight'; an easy way to remember this is to think of it being related to **inflame**. However, you are by no means the only one to be confused, and many people now advocate the use of **flammable** for this meaning, with **non-flammable** for the opposite.

Q I have often seen the word SELF-DEPRECATING used to mean 'self-disparaging, putting oneself down', but none of the senses of *deprecate* in the dictionary seem to fit this. Is the word a mistake?

The term **self-deprecating** has been in use since at least the 1920s to mean 'self-disparaging, self-belittling'. Strictly speaking, it does not correspond to any accepted sense of **deprecate**, but has arisen as a result of the common confusion of this word with **depreciate**. It would therefore be logically correct to use **self-depreciating** or **self-depreciatory**, but **self-deprecating** has become so well established that it is clearly here to stay.

Properly, to depreciate something is to make light of it, to deprecate it is to disapprove of it.

As the previous letter shows, English usage is not an exact science, and sometimes we cannot give a definite answer. It all depends . . .

Q If a notice saying 'No access to main stairs' means that you cannot get to the stairs, shouldn't a notice saying 'No access to staff' mean that you cannot get to the *staff*?!

The construction 'access to' is unfortunately a genuine and insoluble ambiguity in English syntax. Only the context can give guidance as to the meaning in any particular instance. In theory, a sentence containing this phrase may even have three possible interpretations:

Venice may be forced to restrict access to tourists.

is obviously intended to mean 'tourists may only be allowed into Venice under certain restrictions', but logically it could mean 'only tourists may be allowed into Venice', or even 'people may not be allowed to make contact with tourists in Venice'. Usually it is possible to decode even brief notices, though a sign in a prison visiting room saying 'No access to prisoners' might cause confusion.

Q I recently came across the following sentence in a newspaper: *This received widespread if not universal*

***acclaim*. Does this mean 'widespread and possibly even universal acclaim' or 'widespread though not universal acclaim'?**

Unfortunately, there is no way of telling, except by guessing from the subject-matter and the surrounding context. (In spoken English the sense can be conveyed by tone of voice.) The expression *if not* in this kind of sentence may often be completely ambiguous, and the *Oxford Guide to English Usage* recommends that such sentences be paraphrased. If 'if not' means 'though not', then write 'though not': if it means 'perhaps' or 'possibly', then use the clearer expression. If you do mean 'though not', the sentence can be turned round like this: *This received, if not universal, then at least widespread acclaim*. It is regrettable that so many writers are unaware of the potential ambiguity of this expression in writing.

Q Does 'to my knowledge' mean 'as far as I know (but I may be wrong)' or 'as I know for sure'?

Either, unfortunately, and only the context can determine which is intended. Often even the context doesn't help, and one must simply grumble at the author and guess.

7

Why . . .?

Q Why is (the word I want) not in my dictionary?

People are naturally disconcerted when they turn to their brand-new dictionary, or to an old and hitherto trusted one, and cannot find the word they are looking for. They write to us in tones which range from mild disappointment to strong indignation. We take it as a compliment that their expectations are so high, and try to explain why, in each particular case, we apparently failed to live up to them. There are many possible reasons:

Q The title of Gerard Manley Hopkins' first poem is 'The Escorial'. What does ESCORIAL mean, and why is the word not in any of your dictionaries?

Escorial is the name of a Spanish village. The building Hopkins wrote about was the *Monasterio de San Lorenzo del Escorial*, a monastery and state residence built in Escorial by

Philip II of Spain. Most of the Spanish monarchs are buried there.

Strictly speaking, a dictionary is a book about words, and does not include names of places and people unless the name has entered the language. For example, *Dartmoor* will appear as part of the name of the Dartmoor pony or sheep, but not as an area of moorland in Devon or a prison. Proper names—the names of places, people, individual things—are the subject-matter of encyclopedias rather than dictionaries, and although some of our dictionaries (such as the *Oxford English Reference Dictionary*, the encyclopedic edition of the *Oxford Advanced Learner's Dictionary*, and the *Oxford Study Dictionary* for students) do include encyclopedic entries, most do not.

Q Why does my *Concise Oxford Dictionary* give 'Jesus' as a swear word first, and then only afterwards mention Jesus as a historical figure?

COD does not contain encyclopedic entries, and therefore there is no entry for Jesus as a person. However, it does contain a definition for **Jesus** in the sense in which it has been adopted as an English word, and then mentions the person in explaining the origin of the word, as usual, in square brackets at the end of the entry. This explanation is very brief (as the person is not the subject of the entry), and is intended to be factual without presuming that the reader is Christian.

Many people object to the use of **Jesus** as an expletive, but since it is used in this way, we must include it if our record of the language is to be accurate. As a comparison, the entry for **Jeremiah** in *COD* deals strictly only with the application of the word in a general sense ('a dismal prophet, a denouncer of the times'), but mentions the personal name as the source from which it is derived.

Sometimes the missing word was not current, or not sufficiently common for inclusion, when the dictionary was published. The now familiar words ***ambivalent*** *and* ***lovat****, for example, arose in the early years of this century; too late for inclusion in the first edition of the* ***OED****, and therefore not included in some of the dictionaries based on it, such as the* ***Shorter Oxford English Dictionary*** *and early editions of the* ***Concise****. (****Ambivalent*** *was included in the Addenda to later editions of the* ***Shorter****, but few people ever looked for it there.)*

We are often surprised by the age of dictionaries people are using. In the late 1980s one of our editors was shown a battered copy of the ***Little Oxford Dictionary****, still in daily use in a solicitor's office; its appendix of new words included* ***radio****. We were taken to task quite recently by a schoolboy because two words in his 1929 edition of the* ***Concise Oxford Dictionary*** *were not in alphabetical order—we were able to reassure him that the mistake had been corrected in later editions, but pointed out that a dictionary published before World War II, space travel, and decimalization, when Britain had an Empire but few people had eaten a Chinese meal, which would not contain such terms as* ***penicillin*** *and* ***rhesus factor****, let alone* ***DNA*** *and* ***genetic engineering****, was perhaps not adequate for his needs.*

For the dedicated dictionary browser a new edition is a great joy, but sometimes their pleasure in discovering new words is tempered by the loss of the old. Nothing is ever deleted from the ***OED****, and the* ***New Shorter Oxford English Dictionary*** *retains all words in use after 1700, but if our smaller dictionaries are to remain at a manageable size some items must be deleted to make room for new material. One reader asked plaintively, 'Do you have lurking lexicographers who, conscious of publication costs, arbitrarily slash perfectly good words from your pages? Is there a secret society, not necessarily dissimilar to the Wild Buffalo Society in the Flintstones, who snip words at random from dictionaries in order to keep the public buying each new edition?' It would certainly make our job easier if we could simply replace, say, every fifth word, but unfortunately it isn't as simple as that. Nor do we delete old words in favour of new ones just to be trendy; each item, old or new, has to earn its place.*

*Many uncommon or archaic words do not appear in small dictionaries such as the **Pocket**, the **Little**, and the **Mini-dictionary**, and it is not possible to treat items in as much detail—something which our readers do not always appreciate:*

Q In the *Pocket Oxford Dictionary* the word IDES is given in its plural form. Why is it not given in the singular form, as it is in the big Oxford dictionary?

The *Pocket Oxford Dictionary* is a small publication and the space for rare words or forms is limited. The entry for **ides** in the *OED* indicates that the word is very rarely used in the singular form **ide**, so this has not been included in *POD*.

Q As a keen cyclist, I am disappointed not to find terms such as 'derailleur' and 'soigneur' in my *Concise Oxford Dictionary*, and 'drop out' appears only in its rugby sense. Cycling is an environmentally friendly form of transport, and we should all be encouraging it in any way we can.

All the words you mention appear in the *New Shorter Oxford English Dictionary*, but were judged to be too restricted in use for the *Concise*. You could argue, and I would agree with you, that more people cycle than play rugby; but we have to face the fact that cycling, whether competitive, recreational, or as a means of transport, is televised and written about far less, so that the terminology of cycling is less often used.

Please do not think that we are anti-cycling; many of us cycle to work and would gladly share the road with more bikes and fewer cars. But manipulation of the language, or the encouragement of one activity rather than another, is not our job; nor do we think that the appearance of such terms in dictionaries would make any difference.

---

*Incorrect spelling sometimes sends dictionary users on a wild-goose chase. **Pejorative** and **minuscule** have already been men-*

tioned (see p. 64). ***Obstroperous*** *and* ***obstropolous*** *are common misapprehensions for* ***obstreperous****. In small dictionaries this is not a problem, because the word will in any case appear between* ***obstinate*** *and* ***obstruct****, but in the* ***OED*** *a note at the wrong spelling guides readers to the right place. Spellings are subject to change (there are many examples in this book); the larger historical dictionaries will give old and new versions, the* ***Concise*** *will give an archaic spelling if readers are still likely to meet with it, smaller dictionaries, which concentrate on everyday vocabulary, will give only the current spelling.*

Matters of spelling and pronunciation exercise many of our correspondents:

Q Why does the spelling rule '*i* before *e* except after *c*' apply, and why do so many words seem to disobey the rule?

The origin of the spelling lies in the history of English pronunciation and especially that of a number of words, mainly of Old French origin, whose English pronunciation has undergone a marked shift. Until the 18th century, this group of words, including *conceit*, *conceive*, *deceit*, *deceive*, *perceive*, *receipt*, and *receive*, were pronounced with an 'ay' sound, like the standard sound of *-ei-* (/eɪ/ in phonetic characters) in words such as *feign*, *reign*, *rein*, *skein*, *veil*. They all then shifted to the modern 'ee' pronunciation (phonetic /iː/), but their spelling, which follows the Old French, had already become more or less fixed by common custom. They are therefore confusing when compared with words such as *achieve*, *believe*, *chief*, and *field*, which had already settled to 'ee' pronunciations and acquired their *-ie-* spellings while *-ei-* was still pronounced 'ay'.

Although all the words listed above have *-cei-*, a few other words share the same history of changed pronunciation from 'ay' to 'ee' and have '*e* before *i*' spellings even though it is not 'after *c*': *seize* is the most obvious example. *Either* and *neither* also show this pattern, but have also acquired unusual alternative pronunciations. *Inveigle* and *heinous* actually show the shift in process, as they have alternative pronunciations in 'ay' and 'ee'.

Several other words also started out with *-ei-* spellings representing the 'ay' sound, but have ended up with different vowel sounds in modern pronunciation (e.g. *foreign*, *counterfeit*, *forfeit*, and *their*) and so give rise to the rule in its narrower form:

i before *e* except after *c* when the sound is 'ee'.

Ceiling seems to be a special case: this spelling in fact varied with *cieling* until the early 19th century, as the pronunciation was always 'ee', and it may have been the influence of other spellings in *-cei-* which helped to fix the modern form.

Height is an oddity, as it is a compromise between the spelling of one form of the word (originally pronounced 'hate'), and the pronunciation of another (originally spelt 'hight').

Leisure is another oddity, as it seems to have had a variant which underwent the shift from 'ay' to 'ee' along with the *-cei-* words. This was adopted in American English and forms a clear exception to the spelling rule even in its strict form. In British English a variant with a short vowel, rhyming with *pleasure*, was adopted and this is now the usual British pronunciation.

There are, of course, various other ways in which *-ei-* is pronounced, and words of later foreign origin may follow the foreign sound (e.g. *eiderdown* from Icelandic, and *stein*, beer-mug, from German). Some words have a stem ending in *-e* followed by a suffix beginning with *-i-* (e.g. *caffeine*, *protein*, *plebeian*), and it would be quite inappropriate to swap the letters round.

This all goes to show that English spelling does not follow very logical or consistent rules, and each word has its own history of adoption and adaptation into English. The rule about '*i* before *e*' has so many exceptions that it is perhaps hardly worth having the rule at all.

Q Why are two letters sometimes joined together in words like 'encyclopædia' and 'manœuvre'? Is there a word for symbols like this? Are spellings such as 'encyclopedia' American?

The symbol in words such as *encyclopædia* is usually known as an **ae** *ligature* (a ligature being a group of two letters joined together). The *œ* symbol is called the **oe** ligature. Other ligatures are sometimes used to improve the spacing of letters in printing, especially *fi* and *fl*, and in old typesetting fonts there were various other ligatures such as a *&* ligature, and several involving the old 'long s' or *ſ* (see also p. 142).

The letter æ originally occurred in the Old English or Anglo-Saxon alphabet under the name of 'ash' (from the Old English word *æsc*, the name of the tree, which starts with the letter). It fell out of use during the 13th century, being generally replaced by plain *e*. Both æ and œ were reintroduced in spelling Latin and Latinized Greek words during the 16th century, but they tend to be dropped again in favour of *e* as a word becomes fully naturalized (*phænomenon*, for example, giving way to *phenomenon*). Sometimes a spelling with *æ* would be adopted by scholarly writers because it was closer to the Latin spelling and so felt to be more 'correct'. This can be seen from the respective dates of recorded use: e.g. *æstuary* (1706) as against *estuary* (1538), and *sphær* (17th century) as against *sphere* (16th century), this itself a scholarly 'correction' of the older spelling *spere* (13th century). In at least one notable case the adopted spelling was in fact not even correct in Latin: the Latin word *fetus* was spelt with a digraph in error in the 16th century, and the form *fœtus* has persisted ever since, though it is dropping out of technical use. The digraphs tended to survive most often in Latin names (e.g. *Æneas*, *Cæsar*, *Œdipus*, *Phœbe*) and in other words of Latin or Greek origin regarded as rather technical (e.g. *ægis*, *pharmacopœia*).

The tendency to print *ae* and *oe* as separate groups of letters, called *digraphs*, long regarded as an acceptable alternative, has now become dominant. However, the trend towards complete elimination of the digraphs (except in the names and technical terms mentioned above) has also continued. It is more strongly marked in American usage, but is also characteristic of British usage. Forms such as *oeconomy* and *oecumenical* are now scarcely if ever encountered, though *encyclopaedia*, *homoeopathy*, *mediaeval*, etc., are still widely used, and *oesophagus* and *aetiology* still predominate in British use over the American *esophagus* and *etiology*.

Both of these trends are gradually reflected in dictionaries, as for example in the listing of *encyclopedic* and *manoeuvre* by the eighth edition of the *Pocket Oxford Dictionary* (1992), where *encyclopaedic* and *manœuvre* were given as the main forms in earlier editions. (The spelling *maneuver* is still regarded as an Americanism.)

The symbol æ also survives in the International Phonetic Alphabet, representing a vowel sound like that of *cat*.

Q Why is *ph* sometimes pronounced *f*?

The use of *ph* for the *f* sound originated in the conventions of classical Latin spelling. The spelling *ph* was used in Latin words derived from Greek ones containing the letter ϕ (*phi*), which represented an aspirated *p*, i.e. pronounced with a definite expulsion of breath, like modern English *p*. This was distinct both from *f* and the Latin *p* (Greek π *pi*), which represented a sound without this aspiration, closer to *p* in French. The distinction in pronunciation between *f* and *ph* disappeared in later Latin and Greek, but the difference in spelling lingered on in Latin and was perpetuated when words from both languages were borrowed into English.

Some words have switched from one spelling to another. **Fantasy**, for example, comes from the Latin and Greek *phantasia*, but via Italian, in which language *ph* has usually changed to *f*: it is occasionally spelt with a *ph* in English. Other words were changed by medieval and later writers from the original English *f* spelling (derived from French) to reflect their classical origins: examples include **phantom, pharmacy**, and **pheasant**.

A similar history accounts for the pronunciation of *ch* as *k* in some English words (e.g. **chorus, school**), reflecting the Latin use of *ch* for the Greek letter χ (*chi* or *khi*).

Q Why is the River Thames pronounced 'temz' or, if you prefer, why is the river name pronounced 'temz' spelt Thames?

The pronunciation of the name reflects its early spellings. The Latin name was *Tamesis* or *Tamesa*, perhaps from a Celtic word meaning 'dark river' or from an even older root meaning 'to flow'. The vowel in early forms varied between *a* and *e*. Towards the end of the medieval period the name somehow acquired an *h*, which has never been pronounced. Earlier spellings also suggest that the word was sometimes pronounced with two syllables, with the stress on the first (**temm**-ess). The loss of the second syllable is not surprising; you only have to say something like 'temmess side' or 'temmess bank' a few times quickly to appreciate how easy it is to drop the unstressed vowel.

Q Why do we have the two spellings JAIL and GAOL? Is there any difference?

Gaol and **jail** came into Middle English at more or less the same time from two French dialects. **Gaol** represents Norman French *gaiole*, *gayolle*, or *gaole*; **jail** the central and Parisian Old French *jaiole*, *geole* (modern French *geôle*). The Norman French version would have been pronounced with a hard *g*, as in **goat**.

In the 17th century there seems to have been some controversy as to which was the correct form; one quotation in *OED* reads, 'they cannot come to a Resolution . . . whether they shall say Jayl or Gaol'. This now seems to be resolved with a typically British compromise; the word is always pronounced *jail* but is spelt **gaol** in official use. In literary use either spelling may be used. The Americans just use **jail**.

Q Why do some upper-class families begin their names with an *ff* instead of a capital *F*? Is it just an affectation?

In medieval times **ff** was sometimes used by scribes instead of a capital F, and the family name may well have been recorded in this form. As those with wealth and power are far more likely to appear in carefully preserved documents such as deeds, charters, or letters patent, **ff**, showing that one's name was recorded in medieval times, acquired a certain snob value. It is not an affectation (if the spelling is genuine) though one could argue that, if they looked, such families could probably find evidence of a capital initial.

Q Why is *f* used instead of *s* in old-fashioned writing and printing?

The letter that looks like an *f* is in fact a form of the letter *s*, and is usually distinguishable from *f* because it does not have a stroke running right through it, though sometimes it has a little hook or stroke on the left hand side.

This letter *ſ*, known as 'long s', was used in place of lower-case letter *s* (though not capital *S*), except at the ends of words. In words spelt with double *ss*, the second *s* was usually short. The long *ſ* derived from earlier handwriting practice, and was extensively used in printing until the 18th century. It seems to have fallen out of use fairly rapidly during the 1780s and 1790s, though some printers continued to use *ſs* for *ss* even after the long *ſ* had been abandoned for all other purposes.

Q Why is the word *ye* used instead of *the* in names like *Ye Olde Tea Shoppe*, and does it have anything to do with the other old word *ye* as in the carol 'O come all ye faithful'?

The two old words spelt 'ye' are quite unrelated, and their spellings arose in completely different ways.

In Old English from the late 9th century, two letters, the runic letter þ ('thorn') and the letter ð ('eth'), were both used for writing the sounds which we now represent with *th*: the voiceless dental spirant, as in *bath*, and the voiced dental spirant, as in *then*. Eth fell out of use in the mid-13th century, and from about 1400 scribes began increasingly to use the *th* spelling, derived from Latin, rather than the thorn. This was partly due to the fact that the letters þ and *y* had come to resemble each other so closely as to be indistinguishable. For a while a dot was placed over *y* to identify it, but the use of *th* instead of thorn was a much clearer solution to the problem.

The letter thorn was lacking in Continental alphabets, so it was easier for early English printers to switch to *th*, but in a few words such as *the* and *that* the use of thorn had persisted in manuscript use, and many printers used *y* as a substitute. Early texts therefore often use y^e and y^t for *the* and *that*, but the *y* symbol is a substitute for thorn, and was never intended to be pronounced as a *y*. This antique printers' habit gave rise to the pseudo-archaic use of **ye** for **the**, the true meaning of the *y* symbol having been forgotten.

The word **ye** used in hymns and carols really is intended to be spelt with a *y*. It is the old plural form of **thou**, but it was replaced gradually between 1300 and 1600 by **you**, which was originally the plural of **thee**. *Thou* and *ye* were thus originally used for 'you' as the subject of the sentence (like 'I' and 'we'), and *thee* and *you* for 'you' as the object of the sentence (like 'me' and 'us'). As *thou* and *thee* also passed out of use, except in dialect and in poetic and religious contexts, *you* came to be used for all the grammatical forms of the second person, whether singular or plural, subject or object of the sentence.

An interesting development in some dialects, and especially in colloquial American English, has been the reintroduction of plurals of *you* equivalent in function to the old plural *you* and *ye*. The dialect form **yous** or **youse** is used in this way, and so is the American dialect form **you-all** (though both are sometimes used inconsistently for the singular as well). Neither of these seems to show any signs of establishment in formal or standard English, though.

Q Why is the bird name *capercaillie* sometimes spelt *capercailzie*, with a silent *z*?

This curious spelling, seen also in Scottish surnames such as *Menzies* and *Dalziel*, arises from the habit among 16th-century Scottish printers of using the letter *z* to represent the Middle English letter ȝ (*yogh*). This letter was a form of the letter *g* used in Old English, whose shape was borrowed from Irish scribes. When Norman scribes introduced the Continental letter *g* for the sound of *g* in *goat* and *gentle*, the letter ȝ was used in Middle English to represent two sounds: one is now spelt with *y* used as a consonant, as in *year*; the other is usually spelt *gh*, and in most forms of English is now either silent (as in *night*) or transformed to an /f/ sound (as in *enough*). As with thorn þ and *y* (see p. 143), a confusion arose in 15th-century manuscripts between ȝ and *z* (hence the Scottish printers' use of one for the other), and yogh, though still used sparingly by Caxton in the 15th century, effectively died out during the 16th century.

The form *capercailzie* thus really represents a spelling similar to another variant of this word, *capercailye*.

As might be expected in 'a nation of animal lovers', we are frequently asked about words for beasts:

Q Why is there no separate plural for the names of many animals?

Many words for animals come from Old English, and some of these had no special plural, or lost it during the Old English period. Examples of these are **sheep, swine,** and **deer**. Because these animals often occur in groups the words came to be thought of as collective nouns, similar to 'people' and 'cattle'. Treating singular words for animals as collectives was then gradually extended.

Most of the animals which do not take an *-s* in the plural (including fish such as cod, plaice, and salmon; mammals such as deer, antelope, and bison; and birds such as snipe, grouse, etc.) have one or both of the following characteristics: (*a*) they are (or were) caught or killed for food or sport; (*b*) they occur in large flocks, herds, or schools, or are in some way difficult to count. In some cases the *-s* is optional: most people speak of *lions* but a big game hunter may use *lion* as a plural. Some plurals with *-s*, such as *fishes* and *trouts*, are used when the meaning is 'different kinds of fish or trout'.

Q Why is it that common animal names such as 'bird', 'cat', and 'dog' are of Old English origin, but the corresponding adjectives such as 'avian', 'feline', and 'canine' are all from Latin?

These adjectives are all rather academic words, and are part of the vocabulary introduced by scholars, mostly after the Renaissance, from the Latin which was the universal language of European scholarship in all branches of medieval learning. Our first records of *canine* ('doglike'), *caprine* ('goat-like'), and *murine* ('mouselike'), for example, are all from Edward Topsell's *Historie of Foure-footed Beastes* of 1607; *feline* is first recorded in 1681, *equine* in 1778, *bovine* in 1817, and *avian* not until 1870. The native English equivalents, regularly formed from *-like*, tend to have less technical applications.

In many other areas of study, the technical adjectives are Latinate while the nouns are Old English, or at least Middle English. In anatomy, for example, we have *cardiac* for the heart, *gastric* for the stomach, *hepatic* for the liver, *renal* for the kidney and so on.

Q Why, in children's stories, are foxes called Reynard and badgers called Brock?

Reynard represents an Old French personal name *Renart*, itself from a Germanic name *Reginhart*. It was the name of the central character, a fox, in the medieval fable *Roman de Renart*. Reynard was the form used by Caxton in his printing of the tale. In the Germanic name *regin* meant 'advice, counsel' and *hart* meant 'strong, brave, hardy', so it is possible that the name was given to the fox because of the boldness and cunning ascribed to him; however, it is probably more likely that the name had lost its literal meaning by that time.

Brock simply means badger; it is one of the few Celtic words adopted by the Anglo-Saxons.

Q Why are cats, especially tabbies, traditionally called Tibby?

Tibby is a short form of the name **Isabel** or **Isabella**, but we don't know why it is given to tabby cats—it may just be because of the similar sound. There is, however, a rather unsavoury theory about the connection between the name Isabel (or Isabella) and the colour of tabbies. The story is told of a lady who vowed, when her city was under siege, not to change her underwear until the siege was lifted. According to which version you read, this was either the Austrian Archduchess Isabel at the siege of Ostend or Queen Isabella of Castile at Granada. Both sieges lasted a considerable time, at the end of which the lady's underwear might well have been rather 'tabby'. The same story is sometimes said to account for the greyish-yellow colour known as **Isabella** (the date of the first recorded use of this rules out the Archduchess).

I must emphasize that we have no proof whatsoever of this theory, but you may wish to rename your cat.

People do not only question why we leave words out of our dictionaries; they also question why we put them in:

Q Why do you continue to put WELSH and WELSHER in your dictionaries, suggesting that the Welsh are swindlers? As a Welshman, I find this very offensive, and I am sure if you included such racist language referring to other nations you would have the Race Relations Board down on you like a ton of bricks.

But we do! There is probably enough in *OED* to offend every nation on earth, and most sections of society. There are terms such as **Irish** referring to a paradoxical or nonsensical statement, **Dutch courage, Dutch treat**, etc. (see p. 17), **Scotch coffee** (a drink of hot water flavoured with burnt biscuit), **English disease** (once a term for melancholia or rickets, but now usually synonymous with **British disease**, the combination of defects seen as causing Britain's economic difficulties), all of which refer to national stereotypes. There are also derogatory words for men, women, old people, young people, and people of various races, social classes, political opinions, and occupations, as well as terms which are not intended to cause offence but sometimes do (some Black people object to **black** as a negative adjective, as in **black day** or **black-hearted**; many North American Indians would rather be called **Native Americans**; some lesbians reject the term **gay**; some Old Age Pensioners would rather be **Senior Citizens**, while others hate the term; the dislike of some people for terms such as **handicapped, disabled**, and **retarded** has led to them being referred to as 'challenged' in various ways, or as having 'difficulties').

In the case of **welsh**, we do not know whether the term is connected with the Welsh, and we give the origin as 'unknown'. It is possible that it is; the nursery rhyme 'Taffy was a Welshman, Taffy was a thief' dates from at least the late 18th century (**welsh** is first recorded in the mid-19th). Both may have been used rather earlier. One theory, for which there is no supporting evidence, is that the term refers to the Prince of Wales (later George IV) not paying his gambling debts—in which case the link with Wales is tenuous to say the least.

We are sometimes requested to leave words with derogatory connotations out of our dictionaries because of the offence they cause. But if the word is part of the language, it is our responsibility to include it, both to explain its meaning and, where necessary, to indicate that it is offensive. People do not search the dictionary for terms of abuse; they look up words that they have seen or heard to find out more about them. If such terms are included, explained, and appropriately labelled, it at least prevents people causing offence by accident.

Sometimes we would like to be able to comply with such requests. We have had letters objecting to the use of ***spastic*** *as a term of abuse, and* ***schizophrenic*** *to mean 'showing inconsistent or mutually contradictory attitudes or beliefs'. We realize how hurtful the careless use of words referring to medical conditions must be to sufferers and their families, and we hope that accurate definitions of medical terms and appropriate labelling of other uses indicates the difference between the stereotype and the reality.*

Q Why do you put slang and swear words in the dictionary? Surely this just encourages people, especially children, to use them.

A dictionary is *descriptive*, not *prescriptive*. Its aim is to provide information about words, not to act as arbiter of which words people may use. The appearance of a word in the dictionary does not indicate that it is 'approved', or that we think people should use it: it simply records that the word is used, and explains its meaning. You cannot forcibly change the English language by omitting words from the dictionary.

The original complete *Oxford English Dictionary* did leave out some 'four-letter' words, because at the time of publication they were regarded as quite unprintable. However, when the Supplement to the Dictionary was being planned in the early 1960s (around the time that the publishers of D. H. Lawrence's novel *Lady Chatterley's Lover* went to court to defend themselves successfully against the charge of obscenity) it was felt that perceptions had changed, and that the public no longer required dictionary editors to exercise this kind of censorship. (The omission of such terms from early dictionaries did not stop anyone from using them, it just made their history more difficult to trace.)

For general dictionaries, controversial items will be assessed on the same basis as any others. Those in common use will therefore appear in most dictionaries; rare terms, or those restricted to certain kinds of user, will appear in the larger dictionaries. This academic criterion for inclusion does not, of course, apply to books intended for children, and controversial terms are generally excluded from these.

While some of our correspondents object to slang words appearing in their dictionaries, others defend them:

Q Why are some words described as 'slang' or 'colloquial', when they are just as much part of the language as other words?

What makes a word slang or colloquial is simply the way in which people use it (or, more importantly, don't use it). Not all words are felt to be appropriate for every occasion. Most words in the dictionary are not labelled and are considered suitable for all occasions, although in some circumstances they might seem rather formal.

Some language would be considered inappropriate on a formal or solemn occasion, or in writing a business or official letter, but is used in speech or in writing to friends. Such words are labelled 'colloquial' or 'slang', not to denigrate them in any way, but to offer some guidance in their use.

Whatever people's feelings about slang, dialect, and other non-standard language in dictionaries, there is no doubt that many find it interesting, as their letters show:

Q When people are upset about something, they sometimes claim to be SICK AS A PARROT. Why a parrot?

We don't know. The parrot is the latest in a long line of creatures and objects apparently noted for their delicate health or feelings. Those recorded in *OED* include **dog, horse, cat,** and **cushion**; I have also heard **pig** and **rabbit**. **Parrot** is no more illogical than any of these; perhaps it was simply the bird's turn.

Q Why is BLOODY a swear word? It doesn't seem very dreadful.

The origin of **bloody** to give force to an expression is uncertain, but is generally believed to be related to the 'bloods' (rowdy aristocrats) of the late 18th and early 19th centuries; **bloody drunk** (as drunk as a blood) was taken to mean very drunk indeed, and **bloody** was then transferred to other contexts.

Its use as a swear word probably stems from the mistaken belief that it is blasphemous; either referring to the blood of Christ or as a corruption of 'by Our Lady'. Until quite recently it was regarded as unprintable and almost unspeakable, and euphemisms such as **ruddy, blasted, blooming,** etc. were used rather than **b——y**. People were cautious of using it even when referring to blood or bloodshed, as in a **bloody wound** or **battle**. As late as 1964 its use in the film *My Fair Lady* was a subject of comment in the press.

Nowadays most people regard it as fairly harmless. Those who will not use it because it is offensive are probably outnumbered by those who don't use it because it's too tame.

Q The slang BRISTOL for a woman's breasts is, as I'm sure you know, Cockney rhyming slang (Bristol cities = titties). But why Bristols? Why not Liverpools, Cardiffs, Yorks, or some other city?

Rhyming slang arises in informal conversation, and it is seldom possible to trace its origin. However, I can make some suggestions as to why Bristol has been honoured above all other cities in this instance:

1. The phrases of rhyming slang usually have a two-stress rhythm, with the first word having two syllables. A two-syllable city name would be preferred, rather than a name with three syllables or one.
2. The phrase is often based on a familiar idea or name, as in **apples and pears** (stairs) and **Barnet fair** (hair), referring to a large and famous horse-fair held annually in the London borough of Barnet. **Bristol City** is the name of a football team, and would therefore be well known in informal conversation.
3. People tend to like phrases in which a sound is repeated, as the *i* in Bristol City.
4. **Bristol** rhymes with **pistol**—a familiar word for objects that also traditionally come in pairs.

All these factors would favour Bristol, although we shall probably never know the precise origin of the phrase or which, if any, of the above decided the matter.

Q Why is an American ten-cent coin called a *DIME*?

The word comes from Old French *dime* or *disme*, from Latin *decima pars* 'a tenth part'. It was originally used (in the late Middle English period) for a tithe (a tax of one-tenth of annual produce given to the Church), and probably went across the Atlantic with this meaning, later being adopted for the coin worth a tenth of a dollar.

Q I have always called the large, round, yellow-fleshed root vegetable a SWEDE, but my cousins in Sunderland insist that it's a TURNIP and tell me that the Scots sometimes call it a NEEP. Why the difference, and where is the 'border'?

There is no exact border for these terms. However, in general there is a linguistic north–south divide running east to west across the country just south of Yorkshire, and it is quite common for words or spellings to the north of this to differ from those in southern England. The northern forms may be common to England and Scotland, although the Scots often have their own. I shall follow southern English usage and call the small white-skinned vegetable a **turnip** and the large purple-skinned root a **swede**.

The word **turnip** first appeared in English in the 16th century. The second syllable comes from Old English *næp*, later *neep*, from Latin *napus*. The origin of the first syllable is obscure, although it has been suggested that it may be from **turn** or French *tour*, referring to the roundness of the vegetable. Both **neep** and **turnip** were used for a variety of similar root crops, of which the turnip was probably the most common. The swede was introduced into Scotland from Sweden in the 18th century and became known as the Swedish turnip, which in southern England was shortened to **swede turnip** and subsequently to **swede**.

In northern England and Scotland **Swedish** was dropped altogether, and for a while both vegetables were called **turnips** or **neeps**. In time people felt the need to distinguish between the two, and the Scots adopted the term **new turnip** for the turnip, while in northern England the turnip is often, confusingly, called a **swede**. As a southerner who has lived in Scotland I follow southern English usage, except when eating haggis with its traditional accompaniments, bashed neeps and tatties (mashed swede and potatoes).

Q Why is it that some people say they are CHUFFED meaning that they are pleased, while for others it means the opposite?

This confusing word seems to have two distinct origins in different parts of the country, from different local words. **Chuff** meaning 'pleased, satisfied' is recorded from Northamptonshire, Yorkshire, and Leicestershire, and is probably related to an earlier sense 'puffed up, chubby'. **Chuff** meaning 'surly, gruff' is recorded from Cornwall, Devon, Somerset, and Kent, and is related to *chuffe*, a medieval term of abuse. The northern sense is now undoubtedly the dominant one.

Q Why are people from Birmingham called BRUMMIES?

This is due to **metathesis**, a term used in linguistics for the changing over of two sounds or two letters in a word, or of two words in a sentence. There are many words in English where *r* and a vowel have changed places (for example, **third** from Old English *thridda*).

Birmingham is recorded in the Domesday Book as *Bermingeham*. In later documents it appears with various combinations of *r + vowel* or *vowel + r*, including *Bremingeham*, *Burmingeham*, and *Brimingeham*. In time '*vowel + r*' became the accepted spelling, but '*r + vowel*' carries on in the semi-humorous **Brummagem**, which reflects an earlier pronunciation.

Nowadays a citizen will write his address as 'Birmingham' and may even speak of Birmingham—using, of course, a Brummie accent.

Q I live in Chelsea, in the area known as 'World's End'. It's obviously not the end of the world, so why is it called this?

The popular explanation is that this area was beyond the fashionable part of Chelsea, and that you might as well fall off the end of the world as live there. But World's End is quite a common name, given to a field at some distance from the farm or settlement it belonged to. Scholars would call it a **nickname of remoteness**. Distant fields were often given names of foreign cities or countries, such as **Nineveh, Gibraltar,** and **China**; North American states were also used. Some, like **Van Diemen's Land, Botany Bay, Moscow,** and **Siberia** were probably unpleasant or bleak as well as remote; names such as **Egypt** and **California** probably denote fields giving good crops, and well worth the trouble of getting to. Such names are often shown on detailed maps of country districts; names of fields that have been built on sometimes survive in street names.

Many everyday words are taken for granted until someone asks 'why . . .?'

Q Why, when we go upstairs, do we arrive on the LANDING?

In the 17th century **to land** could mean 'to arrive at a stopping place on a journey'—this could be the destination or one of the stages on the way. Arriving at a resting-place on a staircase could be called **landing,** and by the end of the 18th century the resting-place itself was called the **landing**.

Q Why is a HAMBURGER called a hamburger if it is made of beef?

The hamburger is actually named after the German city of Hamburg, and its name therefore has nothing to do with ham. The 'frankfurter' sausage is similarly named after Frankfurt (German adjectives derived from the names of places always end in *-er*). The hamburger was originally called a 'Hamburg steak' or 'Hamburger steak', and was introduced by German immigrants to North America in the middle of the 19th century.

At the beginning of this century, people started using the word 'Hamburger' by itself, and then in the 1930s shortened it even further to 'burger'. As other kinds of food were invented which looked like hamburgers but had different ingredients, the word 'burger' was used to name them (e.g. 'fishburger'). This made it look as though 'hamburger' meant 'burger made of ham', so the replacement term 'beefburger' was invented to get round the problem.

Q One often sees notices, when road-works are in progress, warning of 'heavy plant crossing'. I know this doesn't mean that a large tree is likely to cross the road, but why are bulldozers and cranes called PLANT?

It does seem rather odd that machinery can be called 'plant', and it is difficult to offer an adequate explanation. The word could conceivably come from 'plant' the verb, meaning 'to put something in the ground to start it growing', and could carry the sense 'what is needed to start building works'. This could be compared to the way 'plant' is used for fish-spawn, i.e. 'what is needed to start a colony of fish'.

However, the word is also used more generally of factories or industrial complexes, and so it may have the sense 'equipment which is more or less fixed for the duration of a job'.

Q Why is a shop that sells papers called a NEWSAGENTS?

A newspaper is a commodity with a fixed price and an extremely short selling period. Instead of buying in bulk to sell over a period and adjusting the price to sell at a reasonable profit, as with other goods, the shop acts as an agent, selling papers on the publisher's behalf for a fixed amount per copy and returning any copies not sold. The publisher appoints the agent and promises to maintain a regular supply, usually subject to certain conditions. In practice most newsagents receive their newspapers through a wholesale distributor rather than directly from the publishers they are contracted to.

Q Why are the letters of the ALPHABET in the order that they are? I suppose the order comes from whatever alphabet is the ancestor of our own, but what decided the order of letters in that language?

This is an intriguing but unanswerable question. The ancestor of our alphabet is the Phoenician alphabet of nineteen characters (representing only consonants), dating from about the 14th century BC. Around 1000 BC this was used as a model by the Greeks, who added characters to represent vowels. This in turn became the model for the Etruscan alphabet, from which the ancient Roman alphabet, and subsequently all Western alphabets, are derived. Characters have been added over the centuries, and others lost, according to the need to represent certain sounds, but the basic order has remained the same. Indeed, it may go back to North Semitic, the ancestor of Phoenician, which developed about 1700 BC. In other words, we do it like this because we've always done it like this, but why we did it like this in the first place, no one knows.

Although the order of alphabetical characters has been established for so long, putting words into alphabetical order has been perfected relatively recently. In medieval times this usually consisted of simply putting together all the words beginning with *a*, followed by all those with *b*, and so on. Strict alphabetical order did not become established until after the advent of printing.

Words can be alphabetized in two ways, known respectively as word-by-word and letter-by-letter. In the former, a shorter word will precede all other words beginning with the same sequence of letters, even if the word is followed by another word. In letter-by-letter alphabetization, the characters are considered as a single sequence, with any hyphens and spaces ignored.

Word-by-word	*Letter-by-letter*
American	American
American English	American English
American language	Americanese
Americanese	Americanism
Americanism	American language

Word-by-word alphabetization is used in telephone directories, as it is the better system for dealing with personal names (under the letter-by-letter system **Tomlins, Nigel** would be separated from **Tomlins, Peter** by any number of **Tomlinsons**). Dictionaries use the letter-by-letter system, which ensures that whether a compound word is spelt as one word, or two, or is hyphenated, it ends up in the same place.

8

Curious and interesting facts

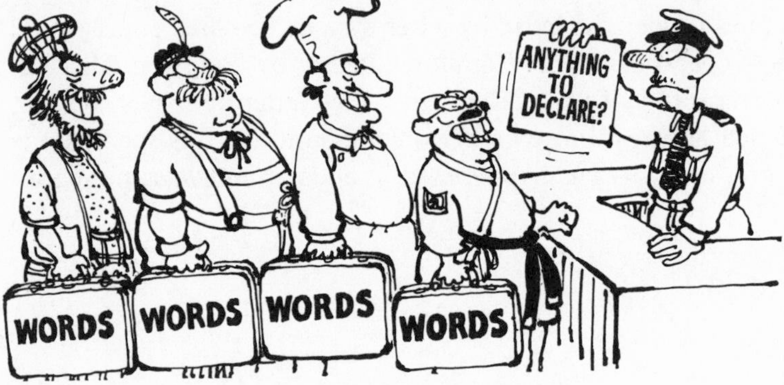

Many facts about the language, while of little or no practical importance, seem to exert a peculiar fascination. Here are some of the most commonly asked questions.

Q How many words are there in the English language?

It is impossible to count the number of words in a language in any meaningful way, mainly because it is difficult to decide what counts as a word. For example: should we count *dog* as one word, or as two (a noun meaning 'a kind of animal', and a verb meaning 'to follow persistently')? If we count it as two, then do we also count inflexions separately, such as the plural noun *dogs* and the present tense of the verb *dogs*? Is *dog-tired* a word, or just two other words joined together? Is *hot dog* really two words, since we might also find *hot-dog* or even *hotdog*?

It is also difficult to draw the boundaries of the English language. As one moves away from ordinary and literary usage, it becomes hard to know what criteria to apply in order to declare a word 'English'. When do technical terms in medical, botanical, or legal Latin start counting as English? What about French words used as terms in cooking, German words used in academic writing, Japanese words used in martial arts? Words used only in broad Scots dialect, or in slang by foreign teenagers? Official systematic names of chemicals? Abbreviations and codes used in computing jargon?

Our best estimate of the number of distinct English words does not count inflexions, and is based on the number of defined entries in the complete *Oxford English Dictionary*. The number of words in use with full entries in the *OED* is 171,476, plus another 47,156 which are obsolete. To this may be added around 9,500 derivative words (such as words ending in *-ness* and *-ly*) which are included as subentries. Over half of the words are nouns, about a quarter adjectives, and about a seventh verbs; the rest is made up of interjections, conjunctions, prepositions, suffixes, etc.

The precision of these figures is to be taken with a large pinch of salt, as they derive from a very simple survey of the computerized version of the dictionary. No account has been taken of the number of entries with senses for more than one part of speech (e.g. both noun and verb). However, this rough estimate suggests that there are, at the very least, a quarter of a million distinct English words, of which perhaps 20 per cent are no longer in use. This excludes grammatical inflexions, and also excludes technical, colloquial, and regional vocabulary not covered by the *OED*. For comparison, Merriam-Webster's *Third International Dictionary* (a major American dictionary) claims a vocabulary of 450,000 words, but this includes many more two- and three-word compounds, phrases, scientific Latin names, and chemical terms. If each distinct sense of each word in the *OED* were to be counted separately, the total would probably approach three-quarters of a million words, over 100,000 of them being obsolete.

The actual number of words used by speakers of English is of course less than this, and varies from person to person, so it is difficult to make even a rough estimate. Also, the 'passive' or 'receptive' vocabulary of words that one can recognize and understand is larger than the 'active' or 'productive' vocabulary of words one can actually use. Hunter Diack, the author of *Standard Literacy Tests* (1976), gives rough estimates of the number of words understood as 6,000 for an able 9-year-old, 18,000 for an 18-year-old, 24,000 for a college graduate, and 30,000 for a middle-aged professional. Other authors have made higher estimates of graduate vocabularies; I think I would expect a graduate to know nearly all the words in the *New Oxford School Dictionary* (which claims 34,000 entries) but certainly less than half of those in the *Concise Oxford Dictionary* (which claims 120,000 entries). Shakespeare's published vocabulary has been estimated at 31,500.

Q Which are the most frequently used English words? Are they 'and' and 'the'?

Several word-frequency analyses have been published, though generally in rather obscure places, each based on the computer analysis of a large corpus or collection of textual material. Three that are quite well known are:

W. N. Francis and H. Kučera, *Frequency Analysis of English Usage* (Houghton Mifflin, 1982), based on the Brown corpus

K. Hofland and S. Johansson, *Word Frequencies in British and American English* (Norwegian Computing Centre for the Humanities, Bergen, 1982), based on the LOB (Leicester/Oslo/Bergen) corpus

J. B. Carroll, P. Davies, and B. Richman, *The American Heritage Word Frequency Book* (Houghton Mifflin/American Heritage, 1971), based on the American Heritage corpus.

All such lists tend to disagree about even the top ten most frequent words in English. To try to compile a combined list is impossible because the methods of analysis differ—for example, some lists combine *to* (the preposition) and *to* (marking verbs in the infinitive); others separate these, but combine tenses of verbs, listing together *be*, *is*, *was*, *were*, etc. A rough top thirty might look something like this:

the of and a to in is that it was he

for as on with his be at you I are this

by from had have they not or one

but *you*, for example, comes 8th in the *American Heritage* list and 32nd in the Bergen list. (We offer no explanation for the appearance of *he* much higher than *she* in the lists!)

Q Can you tell me the relative frequency of the letters of the alphabet in English?

The classic analysis of letter frequencies was made by Samuel Morse (1791–1872), the inventor of the Morse code. He proceeded simply by counting the numbers of letters in sets of printers' type, and came up with the following figures for relative numbers:

12,000	E	2,500	F
9,000	T	2,000	W, Y
8,000	A, I, N, O, S	1,700	G, P
6,400	H	1,600	B
6,200	R	1,200	V
4,400	D	800	K
4,000	L	500	Q
3,400	U	400	J, X
3,000	C, M	200	Z

The mysterious words 'etaoin shrdlu', occasionally seen in newspapers, result from the compositor idly tapping the keyboard, which was laid out in this order, rather than the familiar QWERTY sequence.

We do not have much detail of any later analyses, though the *Guinness Book of Records* once compiled a list very similar to the table above, with *w* and *g* placed between *c* and *m* in the ordering. It would be difficult to compile a body of text which is representative enough to count: for example, a count of letter frequencies in books published by the Oxford University Press would have a relatively high proportion of *z*'s, because of the editorial preference for *-ize* spellings in verbs. An American survey would show a similar number of *z*'s, but would be deficient in *u*'s because of the use of *-or* instead of *-our* spellings.

Q What is the LONGEST WORD in the English language?

The longest word in ordinary use and included in the *Concise Oxford Dictionary* is *deinstitutionalization* (22 letters), though the plural word *counter-revolutionaries* is the same length if the presence of a hyphen is ignored. However, there are many other words of comparable length which are in technical use and are listed in the complete *Oxford English Dictionary*: a list of the longest is given below, each with the date of a genuine example cited in the dictionary (usually the first example).

immunoelectrophoretically	(25 letters)	1961
psychophysicotherapeutics	(25 letters)	1922
thyroparathyroidectomized	(25 letters)	1956
pneumoencephalographically	(26 letters)	1950
radioimmunoelectrophoresis	(26 letters)	1962
psychoneuroendocrinological	(27 letters)	1971
antidisestablishmentarianism	(28 letters)	1923
hepaticocholangiogastrostomy	(28 letters)	1933
spectrophotofluorometrically	(28 letters)	1975
floccinaucinihilipilification	(29 letters)	1741
pseudopseudohypoparathyroidism	(30 letters)	1952
metaphysico-theologo-cosmolonigology	(34 letters)	1759
pneumonoultramicroscopicsilicovolcanoconiosis	(45 letters)	1936

Many of the longest words are inventions, and are almost always cited as long words, rather than actually used. For example, the medieval Latin word *honorificabilitudinitas* (honourableness) was cited by many older dictionaries in its Anglicized form *honorificabilitudinity* (22 letters), but it has never really been in use. However, we do have a few genuine examples of *antidisestablishmentarianism* (see p. 129). We also have genuine if light-hearted examples of *floccinaucinihilipilification* (dismissing as worthless): this word was formed by running together the words *flocci*, *nauci*, *nihili*, *pili* from a line in the Eton Latin Grammar, a standard schoolbook for students of Latin in the 18th and early 19th centuries. *Metaphysico-theologo-cosmolonigology* was the supposed subject of lectures by the character Pangloss in Voltaire's *Candide*. *Pneumonoultramicroscopicsilicovolcanoconiosis* is supposedly the name of a lung disease caused by the inhalation of fine sandy volcanic dust, but it has never been a real medical term. The formal systematic names of chemicals are almost unlimited in length (e.g. *aminoheptafluorocyclotetraphosphonitrile*—40 letters), though longer names are usually sprinkled with numerals, Roman and Greek letters, and various other arcane symbols.

Many of our enquirers seem to have been prompted to write to us by a quiz game or word competition, and some questions have achieved the status of 'chestnuts'.

Q Are there any English words ending in -GRY apart from 'angry' and 'hungry'?

There are certainly no other common English words ending in *-gry*. Apart from oddities such as *un-angry* and *a-hungry*, the next most common is the obscure word *aggry*, as in 'aggry beads', which according to various Victorian writers are coloured glass beads found buried in the ground in Africa. This word has not really become established in English use.

The word *puggry* is also listed in the complete *Oxford English Dictionary*, but it is just one of several 19th-century attempts to spell the Hindi word *pagri* (the usual English spelling is 'puggaree' or 'puggree' and the word means either 'turban' or 'a piece of cloth worn round a sun-helmet'). Other rarities include *iggry* (an old army slang word meaning 'hurry up', borrowed from Arabic) and the archaic spellings *begry* (15th-century—'beggary'), *skugry* (16th-century—'scuggery', a dialect word meaning 'secrecy'), *podagry* (17th-century—'podagra', a medical term for gout), *nangry* (rare 17th-century spelling of 'angry'), *conyngry* (17th-century form of 'conynger', an obsolete word for a rabbit warren which survives in old field names as 'Conery' or 'Coneygar'), *menagry* (18th-century—'menagerie'), and *higry-pigry* (18th-century—the drug 'hiera picra'). There is also the rare obsolete word *meagry* meaning 'meagre-looking', and the *gry* (presumably pronounced to rhyme with 'cry'), the name for a hundredth of an inch in a long-forgotten decimal system of measurement devised by the philosopher John Locke.

Q I'm told that there are three English words ending in -SHION, but I can only think of 'cushion' and 'fashion'. What is the other one?

The third word usually cited is **hushion**, a Scots dialect word for a kind of footless stocking or leg-warmer (also spelt *hoshen* and distantly related to the word **hose** meaning 'stocking' or 'legging'). However, this is not really in general use even in Scotland.

There is, however, a more widely used Scots word: **fushion**, meaning 'spirit, energy, gumption' or (in referring to food) 'wholesomeness'. This word is not used in standard English outside Scotland.

The complete *Oxford English Dictionary* does also list *parishion* (meaning the same as 'parishioner'), but this word never settled down to any particular spelling before it dropped out of use in the 16th century.

Q Are there any English words containing the same letter three times in a row?

The traditional conventions of ordinary English spelling forbid triple letters, and if a compound word would contain three identical letters together, then a hyphen is normally inserted, as in *bee-eater*, *bell-like*, *chaff-flower*, *cretaceo-oolitic*, *cross-section*, *egg-glass*, *joss-stick*, *off-flavour*, *hostess-ship*, *puff-fish*, *toll-lodge*, *zoo-organic*, etc. A person who flees is a *fleer*, just as a person who sees is a *seer*, though because this also means specifically 'person who foretells the future' the forms *see-er* and *seeër* have also been used.

However, it must be said that odd-looking spellings such as *crosssection* are occasionally seen, and the complete *Oxford English Dictionary* does give examples of *frillless* (lacking a frill), of the county name *Rossshire*, and of *bossship*, *countessship*, *duchessship*, *governessship*, and *princessship*. It also lists one extraordinary example of a medieval spelling of *ash* as *esssse* with four s's.

Otherwise, apart from representations of noises, such as *brrr*, *shhh*, and *zzz*, which do not really count as proper words, the only example we have of a triple letter is in the artificially constructed word *Amerikkkan*, a variant spelling of *American* which has been used to symbolize the racist aspect of American society by including the initials of the Ku Klux Klan.

Q Is Y a vowel or a consonant?

It is impossible to give an absolute answer. The terms *vowel* and *consonant* each have two applications, to *sounds* and to *letters*.

The reference to *sounds* is technically the prior one, since speech is prior to writing. A vowel is 'a speech-sound made with vibration of the vocal cords but without audible friction, more open than a consonant and capable of forming a syllable' (*Concise Oxford Dictionary*). The sound of a vowel does not involve any interruption of the airflow by any part of the mouth or throat such as the tongue or teeth, and a vowel on its own can form a syllable without the support of any other sound. A consonant is 'a speech sound in which the breath is at least partly obstructed, and which to form a syllable must be combined with a vowel'.

Clearly, *y* can fit either of these definitions. In words like *hymn* or *myth* it is the *y* which forms the syllable, the other sounds clearly being consonants. The same is true in *by* and *my*, where the *y* stands for a diphthong (a combination of two vowels). On the other hand, in *beyond* there is an obstacle to the breath which can be heard between the two vowels, and is also present in words such as *yes* and *youth*. In terms of sounds, *y* can therefore stand for either a vowel sound or a consonant sound. The consonant sound of *y* is often called a *semivowel* because it is similar to a vowel in the way it is made.

Whether the letter *y* is a vowel or a consonant seems then to be an almost arbitrary decision. It is probably more often used as a vowel, and is regarded as a vowel in the Roman alphabet (having been borrowed from the Greek vowel *upsilon*), but its use as a vowel in English could perhaps be thought of as secondary, since it is often interchangeable with *i* (as in *stile* and *style*, which sound the same). The consonant sound represented by *y* is not consistently represented by any other letter (though it occurs in words like *Europe* and *use*). We might therefore regard *y* as a consonant, just as we regard *w* as a consonant, though it also represents a vowel sound in words like *law* and *new*.

Q Are there any English words which contain the letter 'q' not followed by 'u'?

The letter *q* was adopted in English from the Latin alphabet, where it was only used with a *u* to represent a /kw/ sound. In Old English this sound was written as *cw* (as in *cwene*, Modern English *queen*), but the Latin spelling was occasionally used, and became more frequent under the influence of Norman French, until by the end of the thirteenth century *cw* had died out, though *q* was not used in English spelling in any context other than as *qu*.

Qwerty, derived from the first six letters on the top left of a standard English-language typewriter, has come to be used as a word in its own right to describe a keyboard which has this standard arrangement of keys. However, with the exception of invented trade names (such as *Qiana*, a proprietary name for nylon in the United States, and the Australian airline *QANTAS*), all other words in the *Oxford English Dictionary* spelt with *q* not followed by *u* are foreign words which are occasionally used in English. For example, the *OED* and *NSOED* between them contain the following:

burqa (Urdu & Arabic), also spelt *burka*: a long veil worn by Muslim women

cinq (French), also spelt *cinque*: the five on dice, and a method of bell-ringing

cinqfoil, also spelt *cinquefoil*: a plant with five-lobed leaves, or a design like this

coq (French), also spelt *coque*: a cock's feather in a hat

Inupiaq: name of an Eskimo language

Iraqi: of the state of Iraq (and *Iraqize*, *Iraqization*)

nastaliq (Persian), also spelt *nastalik*: a Persian script

qadi (Arabic), also spelt *cadi*: a civil judge in a Muslim country

qaimaqam (Arabic & Turkish), also spelt *kaimakam*: a Turkish administrator, originally in the Ottoman Empire

Qajar: name of a people of northern Iran

qanat (Persian & Arabic): an underground channel

qanun (Persian & Arabic), also spelt *kanoon*: a stringed musical instrument

Qashgai, also spelt *Kashgai*: name of a Turkic people of Iran

qasida (Arabic): a classical Persian and Arabic verse-form *qat* (Arabic), also spelt *k(h)at*: a shrub grown in Arabia

Qatabanian: of the ancient kingdom of Qataban in southern Arabia

Qatari: of the Arab state of Qatar

Qazaq: a rare spelling of *Kazakh*, name of a people of central Asia

qazi: another spelling of *qadi*

qere (Aramaic): a substitute reading in the Hebrew Scriptures

qi (Chinese), also spelt *chi*: the physical life-force in Chinese philosophy

qibla(h) (Arabic), also spelt *kibla(h)*: the direction in which Muslims pray

qibli (Arabic), also spelt *ghibli*: a southerly wind in N. Africa

Qin (Chinese), also spelt *Chin, Tsin*: name of an ancient Chinese dynasty

qindar (Albanian), also spelt *qintar*: a monetary unit of Albania

Qing (Chinese), also spelt *Ching, Tsing*: name of the Manchu dynasty of China

qinghaosu (Chinese): a drug extracted from Chinese worm-wood

qirsh (Arabic): a silver coin, and now a monetary unit of Saudi Arabia

qiviut (Inuit): the underwool of the musk-ox

sambuq (Arabic?), also spelt *sambuk*: a small sailing boat of the Arabian coast

Shqip, Shqyp: the Albanian word for 'Albanian'

Shqipetar: the Albanian language

suq (Arabic), also spelt *souk*: an Arab market-place or bazaar

talaq (Arabic), also spelt *talak*: divorce, in Islamic law

taliq (Arabic), also spelt *talik*: a Persian script

taluq (Persian & Urdu), also spelt *taluk*: an estate or district
taluqdar: person in charge of a taluq
tranq: slang abbreviation of *tranquillizer*
umiaq (Inuit), also spelt *umiak*: a kind of canoe
waqf (Arabic), also spelt *wakf*: a form of Islamic charitable endowment
yaqona (Fijian), also spelt *yanggona*: the kava plant and the drink made from it
Zindiq (Arabic), also spelt *Zindik*: among Muslims, a kind of heretic

---

Other enquiries are not about words but about dictionaries, and about how words get into them. Some aspects of this are dealt with in the next chapter, but the following letters combine the answers to several similar queries we have received.

Q How long does it take to write a dictionary, and how do you do it?

The time taken to complete a dictionary depends first on its size, secondly on the amount to which it can rely on an earlier edition, and thirdly on the resources and number of editors available. The *New Shorter Oxford English Dictionary* took around thirteen years to write, with a team of up to sixteen full-time lexicographers, plus keyboarders, researchers, file-sorters, and consultants, as well as the usual small army of proofreaders and printers. Smaller dictionaries may be completed in a few years, depending on how much material needs to be revised or written afresh. The original *Oxford English Dictionary* was first planned in 1857, and completed in twelve volumes between 1884 and 1928. The *Concise Oxford Dictionary* was first published in 1911, and its smaller relatives the *Pocket* and the *Little* in 1924 and 1930 respectively.

Preparation for a new edition may be begun at any time

after publication of the earlier edition, depending on the size and popularity of the dictionary, and the availability of staff. After the publication of the *Concise Oxford Dictionary* in 1911, new editions were published in 1929, 1934, 1951, 1964, 1976, 1982, and 1990. Work on a ninth edition is now under way. A new edition must try to cover new vocabulary, including new senses of existing words, and correct any errors or unclarities in earlier editions. The information given in any particular dictionary, and the manner of its presentation, is continually reviewed by the editors.

The production of a bilingual dictionary is additionally complicated by the need to have two editorial teams, one for each language, and to produce each half of the dictionary so as to give the best guidance for translation in each direction between the two languages, while making sure that the halves are consistent with each other.

English dictionaries for learners of English, such as the *Oxford Advanced Learner's Dictionary*, are produced separately by the English Language Teaching Division, as the requirements of learners are very different from those of native speakers of English: much more explanation is necessary, and much more grammatical detail and illustration of usage, which leaves less space for information such as word origins, and prevents the inclusion of more unusual words.

Q How do you decide which words will appear in the dictionary?

All dictionaries have basic criteria for deciding which words should be included, and these generally assume a rule of thumb that the more rarely a word is encountered, the less likely it is that anyone will need to look it up. A major concern in small dictionaries is keeping the book down to a manageable size, so words found only in regional dialects, or in specialist technical works, or in historical texts, are not usually included except in the largest dictionaries, or in specialist dictionaries. Most dictionaries have a particular purpose: our largest dictionaries (the *Oxford English Dictionary* and the *New Shorter OED*) are intended to record the history of English usage, but smaller dictionaries are generally intended to explain only current English, either to native speakers of English (like the *Concise Oxford Dictionary*) or to foreign learners (like the *Oxford Advanced Learner's Dictionary*). It should be noted that obscure words which are scarcely if ever encountered outside the world of word games and crossword puzzles are not regarded as part of the current language.

The Oxford Dictionary Department has an electronic database—a 'corpus'—consisting of huge samples of text, from books, magazines, newspapers, and many other kinds of source. Lexicographers are able to scan and analyse this with the aid of various computer programs to assess which words are in current use, and in what way they are actually being used. The Department also conducts a reading programme, in which readers work their way through texts of various different kinds searching for new or unusual words, or for new uses of well-established words, or even just for ordinary examples of words as they appear in context. Dated quotations are keyed into the database, or added to the several million slips of paper in the files. Around 10,000 quotations a month may be added to the database by the reading team: some of these end up as illustrative examples in the final entry. Words are also brought to the attention of lexicographers by correspondents who send examples of new or unusual words.

When evidence of sufficiently widespread usage has accumulated, the material is forwarded to a lexicographer for drafting, and the word's etymology, pronunciation, meaning, and any important features of its use are researched. We have an extensive reference library, and also have researchers in the Bodleian Library and a number of national, university, and specialist libraries in England, the USA, and Canada. Special consultants in various fields also provide information and additional evidence. Several hundred new words and senses are drafted each year for future incorporation into the complete *OED*, and many are also added to the smaller dictionaries. The biggest growth areas tend to be politics and the environment, health and medicine, computing, and slang.

Q Is there some central committee responsible for assessing proposals for new English words, like the Académie française, which examines and approves new French words?

No, there is no group or body which does this. During the 17th and 18th centuries there was considerable interest in the standardization of English: Daniel Defoe proposed the establishment of an academy 'to polish and refine the English Tongue' in 1697, Jonathan Swift produced a volume entitled *A Proposal for Correcting, Improving, and Ascertaining the English Tongue* in 1712, and Samuel Johnson's famous dictionary was published in 1755. However, though there were some attempts to found an English Academy, they were ultimately unsuccessful.

English is now such a vast and varied language, spoken in such a variety of countries, that it is doubtful whether any institution could have either the authority or the ability to tell English-speaking people what to do and what not to do. New words must simply be introduced and then left to sink or swim. A really useful word is likely to survive this process, though many fairly dubious concoctions will inevitably come into general use at the same time.

Q If a trademark appears in the dictionary without a capital letter, does that mean it is no longer a trademark?

No, it does not mean that at all. It simply means that, as far as we can tell from our evidence, the word is in common use, and is more often seen without a capital letter. This does not itself affect its legal status as a trademark, and dictionary editors are always careful to try and indicate when a word is registered as a trademark or proprietary term.

The owner of a trademark has the right to control use of that trademark for the purpose for which it was registered, but it is not possible to control the ordinary use of language. So the owners of the **Hoover** trademark cannot stop people using the verb *to hoover* for the action of using a vacuum cleaner, though they would like to; but they can prevent other people who make vacuum cleaners from calling them 'hoovers'. Particle physicists have named a hypothetical property of subatomic particles 'technicolour', but this does not affect the proprietary status of **Technicolor** as a trademark in the film industry.

9

I've made up a word

'I took thought, and invented what I conceived to be the appropriate title of "agnostic" . . . and I took the earliest opportunity of parading it at our society, to show that I, too, had a tail like the other foxes. To my great satisfaction, the term took; and when the *Spectator* had stood godfather to it, any suspicion in the minds of respectable people that a knowledge of its parentage might have awakened was, of course, completely lulled.'

T. H. Huxley's claim was verified by R. H. Hutton:

'Suggested by Prof. Huxley at a party . . . at Mr. James Knowles' house on Clapham Common, one evening in 1869, in my hearing.'

We seldom have so much information about the birth of a word. Each must have had a creator, or a godparent who introduced it into English society from abroad, but we seldom know who they were. We know that Lewis Carroll invented ***chortle****, and that the great French chef Escoffier created* ***Melba sauce*** *and named it in honour of the soprano Dame Nellie Melba, but in most cases all we can do is report the first use of the new word in a document which has circulated widely enough and survived long enough for us to know of it. Occasionally the first citation will include an explanation of the word's meaning, as though the writer did not expect the reader to be familiar with it, which suggests that we are close to the source. But usually there are no clues as to the age and antecedents of the 'new' word.*

Sometimes we know all about a new word, because its creator writes to tell us. 'I have invented a word', the letters begin, and most end, 'please will you include it in your dictionary'. The answer to that is 'no'. All Oxford dictionaries are based on usage. A newly invented word is not put into the dictionary until there is clear evidence that it has become accepted into English by a good number of those who use the language. We do not impose words on the language; we are trying to reflect the language as it develops, not to influence its development.

One correspondent asked us if the word could be introduced on the Channel 4 programme ***Countdown****, which relies on Oxford lexicographers to adjudicate. We replied that only words in the* ***Concise Oxford Dictionary*** *were allowed; and that in any case the contestants would never think of the word unless it was already part of their vocabulary. Another offered us the use of his word if we paid him £50,000—it took a little while to compose a polite response.*

Not all the words offered to us are new:

Q I notice in the *Concise Oxford Dictionary* that you include the word WORKAHOLIC. I believe I actually invented this, at a dinner party in (I think) 1970, when I was looking for a word to describe my husband. I have seen it several times lately, and wonder how it got into circulation.

We have numerous claimants for **workaholic** (our first quotation is dated 1968). Words are often created by analogy from terms such as **alcoholic**, **Watergate**, and **neighbourhood watch**: **-holic** can be used for almost any kind of addiction (**chocoholic**), **-gate** for any political scandal (see p. 21), and **-watch** for surveillance or monitoring (**foxwatch**, and recently from the *Independent*, **quangowatch**). These are to a great extent 'words waiting to happen' and may well be invented by several people quite independently of each other. This does not invalidate your claim to have thought the word up, but unfortunately you were not the first.

---

*A little boy wrote, 'I have invented this word. It is called **bodge**.' We had to tell him that the word was already in **OED**, the first quotation dated 1552; a closely related word dated 1519 suggests that it had already been in use for some time. Children often invent words; many just nonsense words that they like the sound of, but sometimes showing a feel for language. The little girl who sent us **floweristic**, meaning 'a person who loves flowers', was aware, consciously or not, that **-istic** forms an adjective which can then be used as a noun. **Shrinkly** (combining **shrivelled** and **wrinkly**), from an 8-year-old boy, is as good as many other portmanteau words. And we were very impressed with the following letter from a primary school in Middlesbrough:*

Q We had a lesson at school about LARGE NUMBERS, but we could not find names for the numbers past a million to the power of 10, so we made some up, using the *Concise Oxford Dictionary* to help us. Can you tell us the proper names, if there are any, and if not, put ours in your dictionary?

They are:

$1,000,000^{11}$	**hendillion**
$1,000,000^{12}$	**dodecillion**
$1,000,000^{13}$	**tridecillion**

$1{,}000{,}000^{14}$	**quadecillion**
$1{,}000{,}000^{15}$	**quindecillion**
$1{,}000{,}000^{16}$	**sexdecillion**
$1{,}000{,}000^{17}$	**heptdecillion**
$1{,}000{,}000^{18}$	**octdecillion**
$1{,}000{,}000^{19}$	**nondecillion**
$1{,}000{,}000^{20}$	**doubledecillion**

There are in fact names for all the numbers you mention (the prefixes deriving from Latin)

$1{,}000{,}000^{11}$	**undecillion**
$1{,}000{,}000^{12}$	**duodecillion**
$1{,}000{,}000^{13}$	**tredecillion**
$1{,}000{,}000^{14}$	**quattuordecillion**
$1{,}000{,}000^{15}$	**quindecillion**
$1{,}000{,}000^{16}$	**sexdecillion**
$1{,}000{,}000^{17}$	**septemdecillion**
$1{,}000{,}000^{18}$	**octodecillion**
$1{,}000{,}000^{19}$	**novemdecillion**
$1{,}000{,}000^{20}$	**vigintillion**

You will notice that you were right about **quindecillion** and **sexdecillion**, and very close to some of the others. Well done!

Others besides children invent words to meet a perceived need. A group of students from eastern Europe, not wanting to use ***boyfriend*** *or* ***girlfriend*** *for those who were 'just good friends', coined* ***friendka*** *for a female friend, restricting* ***friend*** *to males. A gentleman who did not give us his address wrote us a heartfelt letter:*

Q I would like to suggest the use of 'receptioner' (for a man) and 'receptionere' (for a woman), in place of 'receptionist', which has no gender but is often regarded as feminine because the job is usually done by women. I raise

this point because I sometimes perform the duties of a 'receptionist' and I object to the female connotation.

Most names of occupations are neutral with respect to gender, or else the masculine form is used for either sex. The exceptions are those few occupations in which both sexes have traditionally taken part (**actor/actress, schoolmaster/schoolmistress,** etc.) and those done only by women (**nanny, housewife,** etc.). However, as you have found, some occupations have become so much the preserve of one sex that the terms have taken on masculine or feminine connotations.

Your problem is not unique. More and more people are now doing jobs traditionally done by the opposite sex and making conflicting demands on the language to reflect this. Male nurses wished to be promoted to **nursing officer** rather than **sister** or **matron**. Female writers generally reject the term **authoress,** feeling that it categorizes their work as being of interest only to other women. The tendency is towards more neutral terms: **actor** is being used more and more for both sexes, and **head teacher** or simply **head** often replaces **headmaster** or **-mistress**. **Doctress** has never been in regular use, and we have not yet heard any demand for terms such as **bus-driveress** or **lexicographess.**

Eventually your problem will be solved, either by the invention of terms such as you suggest or by male receptionists becoming so commonplace that the word will lose its feminine connotations. In the meantime, I'm afraid, there is very little you can do.

Even when we are in full agreement about the need for a word there is nothing we can do to promote its use. Every time we longwindedly write 'he or she' or 'his or her' in a definition we think of the many neutral pronouns that have been sent to us, or that we have seen suggested, and that now lie in our files—none of them have ever caught on.

We are often asked, 'I have made up a word—may I use it?' The gist of our answer is 'yes, why not—it's your word'. The problem with using a word that does not appear in any dictionary is that you will not be understood, but if you are prepared to be ignored or to be forever explaining yourself, the way to get your word into the language is to use it, and to introduce it to as many other people as you can.

One creator gives a good example of how to promote a word. He took the existing word ***datestone***—*a stone built into the wall of a building, carrying the date of erection or refurbishment. He extended its meaning to include any device with a similar purpose—dates on plaques, girders, lamp-posts, church bells, etc.—and coined* ***datestoneologist*** *and the rather ornate* ***lapiscriptitographer*** *as terms for those who study these date-markers. He used these in a book, in articles in a local history magazine, and on local radio, and he sent us the references. We have heard no more of these words since, but should the study of datestones become popular and the words come into general use, we have the evidence of their origin in our files.*

We have to say that most words that people send in have very little life-expectancy. Many fulfil no need, being alternatives for words already long established, or describing concepts so rare that we have never felt the lack. However, occasionally a new coinage does seem to fill a gap, and we present three words out of the many we have received for your approval:

deceed*: to be less than, the opposite of* ***exceed****: 'Next year inflation is expected to deceed 2 per cent.'*

throth*: all three, equivalent to* ***both****, but used of three things or people: 'Throth of my elder brothers, Peter, John, and Michael went to Oxford.'*

loobry*: the collection of books kept in the lavatory for idle browsing: '****Questions of English*** *is just the book for your loobry.'*

If you think these have some merit and deserve a chance, use them. If enough people use them often enough and for long enough, they may, eventually, get into the language and into the dictionary. It's up to you.

Bibliography and guide to sources

Of the major dictionaries that we use in answering queries, the most important is undoubtedly *The Oxford English Dictionary* edited by J. A. Simpson and E. S. C. Weiner (2nd edition, 20 vols., 1989). This has now been supplemented by the first volumes in the *Oxford English Dictionary Additions Series* (vols. 1 and 2, 1993). We often refer also to *The New Shorter Oxford English Dictionary* edited by Lesley Brown (2 vols., 1993). For dialect words, the most comprehensive source is Joseph Wright's *English Dialect Dictionary* (1898–1905), though this is clearly now very old; a number of counties have local dialect societies which produce more up-to-date glossaries. There is also the multi-volume *Scottish National Dictionary* edited by William Grant and David Murison, and completed in 1976. A more manageable *Concise Scots Dictionary* is edited by Mairi Robinson (1985).

No dictionary can guarantee to help you find a word when you have only the meaning, but possible sources are the

Oxford Thesaurus and the *Oxford Reader's Digest Wordfinder*, or any good thesaurus, and the *Reader's Digest Reverse Dictionary*.

The most useful source for 20th-century slang is Partridge's *Dictionary of Slang and Unconventional English*, now edited by Paul Beale (8th edition, 1984). An entertaining selection is provided in the *Oxford Dictionary of Modern Slang* by John Simpson and John Ayto (1992). A wide selection of vocabulary of the present day, from the colloquial to the technical, is surveyed in the *Oxford Dictionary of New Words* by Sara Tulloch (1992). For phrases and expressions, *Brewer's Dictionary of Phrase and Fable* (14th edition, 1989) is still worth consulting first. Less word-directed queries are sometimes answerable from the *Oxford Dictionary of English Proverbs*, or even *A Dictionary of Superstitions* edited by Iona Opie and Moira Tatem (1989).

Etymology is well covered by the *Oxford Dictionary of English Etymology* by C. T. Onions (Oxford, 1966), E. Klein's *Comprehensive Etymological Dictionary of the English Language* (2 vols., 1966), and Eric Partridge's *Origins* (1958), though some later research is reflected in the etymologies in *The New Shorter Oxford English Dictionary*.

For place names, we make much use of *A Dictionary of English Place-Names* by A. D. Mills (1991) and the earlier but more detailed *Oxford Dictionary of English Place-Names* by E. Ekwall (4th edition, 1960). A more general discussion covering the whole of the British Isles is found in *The Guinness Book of British Place Names* by Fred McDonald and Julia Cresswell (1993). Personal names can be sought in *A Dictionary of First Names* (1990) and *A Dictionary of Surnames* (1988), both by Patrick Hanks and Flavia Hodges, in the more historical *Oxford Dictionary of English Christian Names* by Elizabeth Withycombe (3rd edition, 1977), or in *A Dictionary of English Surnames* by P. H. Reaney and R. M. Wilson (3rd edition, 1991).

Suggestions for Further Reading

For topics concerning language in general, large encyclopedias frequently provide a good introduction, but the *Cambridge Encyclopedia of Language* by David Crystal is devoted to the subject. General information can also be sought in the wide-ranging *Oxford Companion to the English Language* edited by Tom McArthur (1992). *The Science of Words* by George A. Miller (1991) is concerned particularly with the biological and neurological basis of language, and *Language and Society* by S. Romaine (1994) with its social implications. *Language Change: Progress or Decay?* by Jean Aitchison (2nd edition, 1991) deals very readably with the question posed in its title. Other issues dear to many people's hearts are covered in *The Dialects of England* by Peter Trudgill (1990) and *Does Accent Matter?* by John Honey (1989).

Standard works on the history of the English language include *A History of the English Language* by A. C. Baugh and T. Cable (3rd edition, 1978) and the slightly more difficult *A History of English* by B. M. H. Strang (1970). Another good survey is *The English Language* by Robert Burchfield (1985). For a lighter overview, try *The Story of English* by R. McCrum, W. Cran, and R. MacNeil (2nd edition, 1992). Would-be word coiners might be interested in *An Introduction to Modern English Word-Formation* by Valerie Adams (1973).

Books on English usage, correct English, and changing English are almost without number, as are anecdotal books which trace the histories of related words. Detailed and thoughtful discussions of the ways in which particular words alter their use over the centuries are provided by two classics of the subject. C. S. Lewis's *Studies in Words* (2nd edition, 1967) and Owen Barfield's *History in English Words* (1953). A light-hearted look at the obscurer corners of the language is provided by a series of books by Ivor Brown (*A Word in Your Ear*, *I Give You My Word*, etc.), published between about 1942 and 1970 and worth rooting out in second-hand bookshops.

For those seriously interested in dictionaries, we would recommend *Caught in the Web of Words: James A. H. Murray and the Oxford English Dictionary* (1977) by K. M. Elisabeth Murray, and *Dictionaries: The Art and Craft of Lexicography* by Sydney Landau (1984). A more informal approach is adopted by Israel Shenker in *Harmless Drudges: Wizards of Language—Ancient, Medieval and Modern* (1979). Anyone who wants to find their way around the *Oxford English Dictionary*, and understand both the depths and the limitations of what it has to offer, might well look at *A Guide to the Oxford English Dictionary* by Donna Lee Berg (1993).

The grammar book we most often reach for is probably *A Comprehensive Grammar of the English Language* by R. Quirk, S. Greenbaum, G. Leech, and J. Svartvik (1985). However, it is very dense, and more everyday queries may be answered in *Oxford English* by I. C. Dear (1986), the *Oxford Guide to English Usage* by E. S. C. Weiner and Andrew Delahunty (2nd edition, 1993), or *English Grammar for Today* by G. Leech and others (1982). The classic usage guide is still *A Dictionary of Modern English Usage* by H. W. Fowler (1926; 2nd edition, ed. by Sir Ernest Gowers, 1965), but it is now a classic, in many respects overtaken by the passage of time. (Dr Robert Burchfield is preparing a new edition.) A user-friendly guide to some common grammatical problems, bizarrely illustrated with old engravings, is provided in *The Transitive Vampire* by K. E. Gordon (1984). For punctuation, try *You Have a Point There* by Eric Partridge, or *Mind the Stop* by G. V. Carey; for pronunciation any large dictionary, or *Everyman's English Pronouncing Dictionary* by Daniel Jones (now in its 14th edition), or Robert Burchfield's *The Spoken Word: A BBC Guide* (1981).

The Lore and Language of Schoolchildren by Iona and Peter Opie (1959) provides a fascinating insight into children's language, and *Indian and British English* by P. Nihalani, R. K. Tongue, and P. Hosali (1979) discusses the way in which English is distinctively used in the Indian subcontinent.

Index